∼How to Write∼
WEDDING
SPEECHES
& TOASTS

How to Write WEDDING SPEECHES & TOASTS

Barbara Jeffrey and Natasha Reed

foulsham
LONDON • NEW YORK • TORONTO • SYDNEY

foulsham

The Publishing House, Bennetts Close, Cippenham,
Slough, Berkshire, SL1 5AP, England

Foulsham books can be found in all good bookshops and direct from
www.foulsham.com

ISBN: 978-0-572-03453-5

Printed in Great Britain by Creative Print and Design (Wales), Ebbw Vale

Contents

Introduction

Congratulations! Someone you know – or perhaps it's you yourself – has taken the plunge and decided to tie the knot. As happy as you are about this, you have probably just realised that one of your duties will be to make a speech or toast for the happy couple and this is quite a daunting task, no matter how confident you may be normally. You have to appeal to a wide-ranging audience, be careful to thank everyone appropriately, be humorous without offending anyone and somehow convey your sentiments without sounding schmaltzy.

Before you know it, everyone will have a piece of advice for you, ranging from 'Don't forget to mention how Bill fell through the window – that was so funny!' to 'If you mention any of Daniel's ex-girlfriends, I will kill you!' If you are not careful, you can drive yourself crazy trying to come up with the perfect speech.

But help is at hand. Firstly, remember that it is not difficult to make a wedding speech. They are relatively short and by the time you are ready to start, the audience will be warmed by the happiness of the occasion and will not expect or want lengthy, slick, professional performances. Don't worry if you are not a great public speaker; everyone at the event will be friends and family and there to enjoy the day, not heckle the speechmaker. All you need to do is relax and do some preparation beforehand. With the knowledge of a few elementary rules, good advice, some preparation and a little practice, there is absolutely no reason why anyone cannot make a great job of it.

This book brings you invaluable information about the traditions of weddings, as well as more modern practices. As weddings become more personalised and unusual, so, too, can the speeches. From slide show photographs of the couple to zany props, speeches are now far more about the married pair than sticking to a rigid format. Whether you are the bride's father, a relative of the bride, the bridegroom, the best man or woman or even the bride, for traditional style or contemporary chic, this book contains everything you will need to make the perfect speech or toast.

So good luck and enjoy your successful speech!

Speechmaking

Whether or not you decide to stick to the traditional format, it is helpful to know the sequence that most people use for their wedding speeches. It is clear and logical, and ensures that all the right people are acknowledged. So even if you are having a more informal or unusual form of celebration, take a look through this chapter to find the basics, then amend it to suit your purposes.

Who says what and when

The purpose of wedding speeches is to congratulate the couple, wish them well in their future life together and to thank appropriate people. They include the toasts, which usually occur after the last course of the meal, and are followed by the cake-cutting ceremony.

Wedding speeches can be daunting, and if you have to give one it can occupy your thoughts even more than the actual ceremony, which, of course, is not the point. But try to relax and imagine that you are just telling a story at a large dinner party. Remember, the 'audience' does not expect, or want, a long and serious oration. They simply expect a few sincere and perhaps amusing words from the speakers and the toasts so that they can get on with enjoying themselves. The speeches are not the most important part of the wedding, and if the speaker prefers, he or she need only say a few words.

If the person planning the wedding makes sure everyone knows the running order beforehand, you will feel more reassured about exactly when and where you have to do your bit. The traditional time for wedding speeches is after sitting down to eat. However, a modern practice that is on the increase is to have the speeches before the meal, as many people prefer to get them out of the way so that they can enjoy the food without worrying! Sort out details such as whether there will be a microphone available or whether you be in a small space where people can hear you easily, which order will you go in, whether a toastmaster or the best man will announce the speeches, and so on.

This book outlines the etiquette of making a speech at any wedding, from a traditional English wedding to one of different faiths and cultures. If different people are to be asked to give a speech (see Modern Toasts, page 16), this can be incorporated; just work out when everyone will say their piece. Beware of fitting in too many speeches, though. You will find that when the groom's mother's best friend's auntie gets up to thank everyone for their thanking her for helping to do the flowers, people will start to fall asleep!

If you are in any doubt at all as to which type of wedding is being planned, you are strongly advised to discuss what will be required of you before you start preparing your speech.

Traditional English wedding

The traditional English wedding reception may be formal, semi-formal or relaxed, with many guests or with just a few. It may be held in a hotel, hall, restaurant or at home. The speeches made at such receptions are expected to be quite short – each lasting for at most four or five minutes – and they involve either proposing a toast or replying to a toast. Usually, they are made after the wedding breakfast – whether a set meal or a buffet – has been taken and before the wedding cake is cut. Incidentally, when a toast is proposed, all who are able, stand and raise their glasses to the person or persons being toasted, who remain seated.

At larger receptions, a professional toastmaster may announce guests and that 'Dinner is served', introduce speakers and announce the cutting of the cake. Generally, however, brief introductions to the speeches are made by the best man.

The order of speeches and content is quite logical. The opening speech is made by the bride's father; he is followed by the bridegroom; finally, the best man speaks. To start off the proceedings, the toastmaster or the best man asks for silence and introduces the first speaker.

Bride's father

If the bride's father is absent for any reason, the speech could be made by whoever has given her away, or by a mature family relative or friend. The specific content obviously depends on the relationship of the speaker to the bride, but assuming that it is her father who speaks, he will do so on behalf of his wife and himself, and may express:

- A welcome to the groom's parents, relatives of both families and other guests;
- How proud they are of their daughter;
- A story about the events leading up to the wedding;

- A story about the bride's earlier life;

- Congratulations to the groom;

- Happiness in getting to know the groom and his family;

- Confidence in the couple's future together;

- A few words of wisdom to the couple for the start of their future life together;

- That they are sure that all guests would want to join them in wishing the couple well;

- The toast to 'the health and happiness of the bride and groom'.

Bridegroom

The groom speaks on behalf of his wife and himself. His speech is mainly to thank people who have been involved in setting up the wedding. He may express:

- Thanks to the bride's father for the toast;

- Thanks to the bride's father for his daughter's hand;

- Thanks for the wedding and reception;

- Thanks for the words of welcome into the family;

- His own happiness and how fortunate he is to have such a lovely bride;

- Praise for the bride's parents on having brought up their daughter so well;

- His luck in joining his wife's family;

- Thanks to his own parents for his upbringing;

- A response to any advice given by the bride's father;

- An amusing story about how he met his bride or any problems that have been overcome;

- Thanks to the guests for attending, and for their good wishes and generous gifts;

- Thanks to the best man, ushers and any helpers;

- Admiration for the beauty of the bridesmaids and gratitude for their participation;

- His wish to present the attendants with gifts;

- The toast to 'the bridesmaids'.

Bride

More and more these days, the bride might to want to say a few words. It is, after all, her day, too. There are no set rules for a speech from the bride, but it can be slotted in after the groom has spoken, or perhaps the bride and groom would like to give a joint speech so they can thank people together. She may express:

- Thanks to all the attendants, together with her new husband;

- Thanks to her father for all his kind words (in this case her speech will need to follow her father's speech);

- Her happiness and how fortunate she is to have such a wonderful husband.

Best man

The best man's speech is always the most anticipated, so it is generally saved until last, with perhaps the chief bridesmaid or matron of honour speaking just before him. The best man responds on behalf of the bridesmaids. As most of the necessary thanks have been given, he has the opportunity to entertain the guests with witty comments and funny stories. He may express:

- The bridesmaids' thanks for the toast and for the gifts;
- A few of his own compliments to the bridesmaids;
- Admiration for the bride, and the groom's luck in having such a lovely bride;
- Congratulations to the bride and groom;
- Pleasure in carrying out his duties;
- A toast to the bride and groom's future happiness;
- His and the guests' thanks to the host and hostess;
- A toast to the host and hostess;
- A toast to absent friends;
- The sentiments and senders of any messages and telemessages;
- The programme for the rest of the reception.

Unusual situations

This traditional order and content of speeches is fine in an ideal world. But, in today's world, how many weddings are there that take place within an ideal, 'happy families' environment? Here are some hints and tips for the more unusual or unconventional weddings.

Second marriage

Speeches and toasts at a woman's second marriage are subtly different from those at first weddings. The toast to the bride and groom may still be given by the bride's father, but this is fairly unusual. He is not, after all, giving his daughter away in marriage this time. Normally, this toast will be made by a male friend, perhaps the husband of the bride's woman friend who sent the invitations for her, or the toast may be made by the best man, if there is one. There are sometimes only two speeches: the proposal of the new couple's health and the bridegroom's response. These speeches need to be suited to the particular occasion. It is bad form to refer to the bride or bridegroom's earlier marriage. See also page 121.

Absent figures

Perhaps one of the bride or groom's parents or family is dead. You will probably want to raise a toast to absent friends and family or mention them in one of the speeches. Be careful to speak to the relatives or friends of anyone being mentioned beforehand though, to make sure that there are no difficult situations whereby the remaining parties don't wish the deceased to be publicly honoured or remembered. The last thing you want to do is offend anyone. At the end of the day, however, it is your speech, so pay your affections to whomever you want to, as long as you are tactful and sensitive to others' feelings.

Divorce

Perhaps the bride or groom's parents have divorced and remarried. If this is the case, take care to mention the new partner(s) if they have played a hand in the wedding and have been part of the couple's life. As with the deceased, mentioning or not mentioning certain people could cause offence, so agree the official line in advance with the couple and the other speakers.

Lesbian and gay weddings

Civil partnership is a new legal relationship that can be formed by two people of the same sex. It gives such couples the opportunity to obtain legal recognition of their relationship. There would be no call for speeches at civil partnership registration, because just like a civil marriage, the process is separate from any kind of ceremony. If you did want to have a more spiritual ceremony, you could always arrange a separate humanist or other type of wedding ceremony that would have special meaning to you. In this case, you could have the speeches and toasts as you wished.

Other situations

Have the bride and groom been living together for some time before deciding to wed? Has either of them been coping as a single parent? These are all possibilities in the real world, so before you write your speech, make tactful enquiries and seek advice from those arranging the wedding.

Modern toasts

As well as the traditional speakers, it is becoming more common to have some other speech-givers too.

- Sometimes the chief bridesmaid will also want to toast the couple. She could speak just before the best man.

- A distinguished guest may be invited to speak at some length. This can be fitted into the order wherever it seems the most appropriate.

- In the absence of a bridal party member, there may be a stand-in speaker, such as a stepfather, a godmother or a brother in place of a father who couldn't be there. The stand-in should acknowledge the absent person and thank people/congratulate the couple on their behalf.

- There may be a best woman instead of a best man. This would obviously take the place of the best man's speech.

- There may be two or even three best men; they could either give a joint speech or go one after the other.

Different cultures and faiths

Different cultures and different faiths have their own traditions.

- For example, at Jewish weddings, often the groom speaks after the best man and the final toast may be to Her Majesty the Queen.

- Scotland has its own customary order of speeches, but this is not always followed strictly.

- Irish weddings may be different again, unpredictable both for the number of speakers and for how long they go on.

- Caribbean weddings tend to be exuberant festivals of colourful clothing and local music, sometimes with little regard to the time of day or ideas of being there on time.

- Asian weddings usually follow a clearly defined pattern particular to each faith, where everybody knows how things are done.

- Interfaith marriages are on the increase, and may involve two weddings, so the parties have to make their own rules about speeches.

2 Researching and Writing your Speech

To many people, writing a speech is a terrifying – or at best daunting – prospect. However, if you obey a few very elementary rules and heed some guidelines, you can succeed with comparative ease.

Researching your speech

Before you start thinking about how to set out the speech, you need to decide what you are going to include in it. Jot down ideas whenever you get inspiration – even if it's on the bus on the way to work – and start to collect some themes and ideas. It is a good idea at this point to speak to the family and find out if there are any facts or people you definitely should or should not mention, before you start creating jokes around them.

Quick questions

Here are some things to ask yourself that might help when preparing the speech:

- How long have you known the couple? How did you meet?
- How did they meet each other? Was it through you?
- How did he propose? What was her immediate reaction?
- How long have they been together?
- Do they have children?
- Are there any mutual interests they share?
- What three words come to mind when you think of the groom?
- What three words come to mind when you think of the bride?

Where to find material

If you have some ideas but don't know how to make them relevant or humorous, there is plenty of material available to help you write your speech, such as books and websites. This book contains lots of great material to start you off; Chapters 7 and 8 (pages 83–124) contain some specimen speeches to give you a starting point. Don't forget to change the names and facts to suit!

Using the basic format, you could take out the chunks that don't apply or that you don't like and add material of your own. If you change the content of a specimen speech, however, do keep the continuity or flow of sentences and style.

Friends and family are good for offering advice, too, but take all their input as just that – advice. Use what you think is sensible and ignore the rest.

Searching the web

The internet contains a whole host of information available on speech writing – just typing 'writing a wedding speech' into the search engine Google results in over 200,000 hits. In the event that you are a technophobe, it's worth asking someone to help you. We have provided some great websites to use as a starting point (see page 21) so that you can begin looking for ideas.

The important thing, however, is not to get carried away with all the information out there. You must be selective and choose material that is appropriate to your particular wedding. Don't just copy speeches wholesale as they will lack originality and won't sound either natural or personal. Another no-no is to include too many jokes. You are not doing a stand-up routine; try to combine sincerity and anecdotes with the odd joke.

Also, a lot of websites will charge you to look at them or will offer personalised speeches for money. You don't need to pay for a speech when this book contains everything you need to know!

Using quotations and jokes

One-liners, jokes and famous quotes are great for adding humour and sentiment to a speech. Chapters 3 and 4 (pages 29–69) contain some quotations, toasts and jokes that may appeal to you. Try not to pepper the speech with other people's words or they will lose their impact. Just choose one or two that are relevant to the couple. If you want to use your own jokes, keep it relatively clean and don't assume inside knowledge on the part of the guests. In-jokes may be really funny to you and the groom, but if only you two and some university mates will understand them, then you could start to lose the guests' attention. Don't, for example, assume that everyone knows that the bride is scared of clowns – if it's worth telling, it's worth telling from the beginning. Go for stories that everyone can enjoy.

Internet inspiration

Check out these websites for ideas and tips.

■ **www.confetti.co.uk** Offers free planning advice for the big day. The wedding speeches section (under Weddings) contains tips, sample speeches, toasts and an A–Z of jokes and one-liners.

■ **www.hitched.co.uk/speeches** Offers a free service offering advice on every aspect of getting married. Here you can find quotes, readings, delivery tips and example speeches for the bride's father, the bridegroom and the best man.

■ **www.presentationhelper.co.uk/wedding_speech.htm** Offers articles and free advice on writing speeches, as well as example speeches for the whole wedding party, including the bride and maid of honour.

■ **www.youandyourwedding.co.uk** Created by one of the UK's best-read wedding magazines, offers features, advice, chatrooms and all kinds of up-to-date information.

One word of caution. If you are not a natural joke-teller, test out your material beforehand so you ensure a slick delivery and don't stumble over the punchline. A simple joke delivered well will be much more effective than a complicated one that lacks style and good delivery.

Writing your speech

You should, by now, have collected together as many facts and details about the wedding as you can. You should also know what those arranging the wedding would like you to cover, and what they would prefer you not to mention, in your speech.

The first rule is always to remember you are writing for speaking, not writing for reading. This is vital if you are to produce a good speech. There is an unfortunate tendency among the inexperienced to come up with a piece of literature – rather like a school composition, or a report to the boss – instead of a speech. Indeed, it has to be said that many books of ready-made speeches on the library shelves are for reading, not for speaking.

Although you won't want your style to seem slovenly, you needn't aim at the finer points of good grammar. In fact, if you do, you'll sound incredibly stilted. Use short sentences. If you don't, you'll very likely find yourself gasping for breath when you deliver your speech. Sentences beginning with 'and' or 'but' are fine, because we begin sentences in that way when we speak. Never use a long word if you are not comfortable with it; you'll very likely stumble over it on the day! On the other hand, try to avoid slang and dialect words and phrases. You may think these relax your style, but your audience might be uncomfortable with them.

Beginning, middle and end

The second rule seems to be stating the obvious: speeches must have a beginning, a middle and an end. How many of you know you could produce a good speech, if only you could get started? So, don't 'get started', begin in the middle! Then you can develop your notes to add your introduction and conclusion. Redraft as often as you like until you are happy with your basic outline.

List all the points you wish to make, and note any outstanding queries you may have. The lists for the three traditional speakers might look something like the following.

Bride's father

Welcome everybody / Thank helpers / Say how beautiful Sarah looks / Sarah's career / How proud we are / Welcome and praise John / Advice to them – perhaps quotation? / Wish them happiness / Toast.
Queries: Call him John or Jonathan? / Check if any of John's close friends or relatives are seriously ill.

Bridegroom

Thank Patsy and Andy for reception / Thank Andy for toast / Thank him for welcome into family / Thank mum and dad for all they've done for me / Thank David for being best man (Joke at his expense?) / Say how Sarah and I met and how lovely she looks / Praise the bridesmaids / Toast bridesmaids.
Queries: Check with Sarah that my joke is OK / Any feuds in Sarah's family to be aware of?

Best man

Thanks for toast to bridesmaids / Thanks for gifts to them / Thanks that I'm best man (Joke) / Admire Sarah / Talk about John (Joke) / Wish them well (Quotation?) / Thank Patsy and Andy on behalf of guests.
Queries: Names of bridesmaids and how to pronounce them / Are they getting gifts? / Check if I'm to read messages / Is Sarah going to speak? / Check if there are any sensitive areas, in either family, to beware of / Check who will introduce the speakers.

Begin your first draft

Once you have your structure, the next step is to make a draft of the speech. Cross off the items on your list as you include them. Remember to use short sentences, an easy style for speaking, and to make your text flow. If you need help with the wording, the specimen speeches in Chapters 7 and 8 (pages 83–124) may help you, and there are other ideas in Chapters 3 and 4 (pages 29–69).

When you feel that your draft is reasonably to your liking, do a rough word count. Something of the order of 450 to 500 words for the middle and end sections will give you a speech of around four to five minutes. If it's much too long, edit out any repetitions and sentences that are not necessary, but still maintain your continuity. If it's still too long, it probably means you have a lot to say and, as long as it's not boring, a slightly over-long speech is no problem – you'll just be speaking for longer, that's all! If your draft is too short, why not add a suitable quotation or joke? But do make it fit naturally into your text; it shouldn't sound as if it is padding for a short speech!

Now it should be a fairly easy task to write in the start of your speech. You have tradition to fall back on if you can't find inspiration to be original. 'Ladies and gentlemen' is the accepted opening, provided there are no guests of higher standing, in which case, for example, 'My lord, ladies and gentlemen', or 'Reverend Green, ladies and gentlemen', should be the form used. Then, say something that will encourage your audience to listen to you.

If you are proposing the toast to the bride and groom, speak directly to the guests. Welcome them, perhaps mentioning some by name. If you are the bridegroom, your guests will expect you to say you are nervous and that you are a lucky chap. If you are the best man, you can thank the bride and groom – in a humorous fashion if you like – for choosing you as best man. If all else fails, the ideas for opening lines that follow are yours for the taking. Choose something that you feel comfortable with, and that will get you off to a flying start.

Some ideas for opening your speech

'Ladies and gentlemen – I'm nothing if not original!'

'As Henry VIII said to each of his wives in turn, "I won't keep you very long."'

'Ladies and gentlemen – you were expecting me to say that, weren't you?'

'It is a great honour for me to be the first one to toast the lovely couple today.'

'Ladies and gentlemen, this is the happiest day of my life. What makes it so, is the lovely girl sitting next to me.'

'Ladies and gentlemen, the bridegroom is expected to say that this is the happiest day of his life. So, tell me, all you husbands listening, does that mean my happiness is on the way downhill after today?'

'Before I begin, please can we ensure that all the
aisles and fire exits are kept clear throughout
the reception. There's a medical team waiting
outside the building and I'd like them to have a
clear run when my father is presented with the
final bill.'

'Friends, I'm not going to say very much, except
that life is full of surprises, and my husband Jake
is the best surprise that's ever happened to me.'

'Ladies and gentlemen, I'm sure you know the
three cardinal rules for after-dinner speakers:
stand up, speak up, then shut up. Well I shan't
disappoint you, I'll do just that.'

'Ladies and gentlemen, when I told my new
father-in-law a few hours ago that I felt nervous
about making this speech, he said: "Don't
worry, everyone expects a groom to make a
complete fool of himself, they'll be disappointed
if you don't." And the last thing I want to do
today is disappoint you!'

Setting out your speech

When writing your speech, make sure you set it out so that it is easy to read at a glance. Typing it out is the best idea as it will avoid any of those 'can't read my own handwriting' awkward pauses. Use a clear font, such as Helvetica or Times New Roman, in a large size and double-space the typing. When people get nervous, sometimes their eyesight becomes blurred and it can be hard to read, so make it easy for yourself.

The content of your speech is not just the words, it is also its shape and structure. On your script, use a coloured felt pen to mark all the paragraph starts and the places where your theme changes.

Use a different colour to mark in pauses, where you will pause for effect or for an expected laugh or other reaction from your audience. Pause markings are invaluable in your speech presentation. You will be able to see a little ahead, just where you can, for instance, clear your throat or take a sip of water, without breaking the flow of your words.

When your draft speech is complete, keep it with you and look at it from time to time, perhaps polishing or improving it as you get new ideas. Have a word, if you can, with the other speechmakers at the wedding, so that you don't duplicate a joke or quotation and so that you know if some point will be raised to which you should reply or react. But keep the speech flowing!

Do...

Your research beforehand. Find out about any family feuds or awkward situations to make sure you don't put your foot in it.

Take it easy on the bubbly – at least until after your speech. A bit of Dutch courage is fine, but don't *drink* too much or you may *say* too much.

Keep it brief – go on for too long and you will lose the attention of your audience. Guests don't want a lecture, so time yourself and make sure you don't go over your limit, even if you are getting a great reception. Always leave the audience wanting more.

Don't...

Discuss only yourself. Talking consistently only about your own wedding day is dull and rude. You can mention something about your relationship with the bride or groom, but only to introduce something interesting about the happy couple.

Be inappropriate. Be careful not to offend your audience and remember that any jokes have to be suitable for both little and big ears.

Mention prior marriages or relationships. Whilst you may think it is hilarious to joke about the bride or groom 'finally getting it right', it will only create awkward or hurt feelings. This is about the happy couple only, so celebrate that.

CHAPTER 3

Using Quotations and Toasts

Quotations live on because, out of their original context, they are witty, pithy, apt, funny, cynical or even unkind. An appropriate quotation, neatly led into, will add a touch of flavour, purpose and shape to your speech, although more than one will probably sound pretentious in a fairly short speech. Never include an unkind quotation or toast in your speech, and do consider that what you find very funny may be hurtful to someone listening to you.

Throw your quotation in lightly, develop on the theme, and if you know its source, tell your audience.

Cynical quotations may be used to good effect, but the speaker should immediately distance the company present from such sentiments.

Here are some quotations that may appeal to you, separated into themes for ease of use.

On marriage

*By all means marry. If you get a good wife, you
will become happy – and if you get a bad one,
you will become a philosopher.*
Socrates

---

*The Japanese have a word for it. It's Judo – the
art of conquering by yielding. The Western
equivalent of judo is, 'Yes, dear.'*
J. P. McEvoy

---

*God, the best maker of all marriages, combine
your hearts in one.*
William Shakespeare

---

*Most girls seem to marry men who happen to be
like their fathers. Maybe that's why so many
mothers cry at weddings!*
Jenny Éclair

---

*There is no more lovely, friendly and charming
relationship, communion or company than a
good marriage.*
Martin Luther

Marriage is a sort of friendship recognised
by the police.
Robert Louis Stevenson

———————————

Marriage means commitment. Of course,
so does insanity.
Anon

———————————

Marriage is a wonderful institution, but who
wants to live in an institution?
Groucho Marx

———————————

Why are women so much more interesting to
men than men are to women?
Virginia Woolf

———————————

Marriage halves our griefs, doubles our joys and
quadruples our expenses.
G. K. Chesterton

———————————

To keep your marriage brimming with love in
the wedding cup, whenever you're wrong, admit
it; whenever you're right, shut up.
Ogden Nash

———————————

For in what stupid age or nation,
Was marriage ever out of fashion?
Samuel Butler

———————

Two souls with but a single thought. Two hearts
that beat as one.
Friedrich Halm

———————

Any man who says he can see through women is
missing a lot.
Groucho Marx

———————

It took great courage to ask a beautiful young
woman to marry me. Believe me, it is easier to
play the whole 'Petrushka' on the piano.
Artur Rubinstein

———————

Love and marriage, love and marriage, go
together like a horse and carriage.
Sammy Cahn

———————

Two such as you with such a master speed
cannot be parted nor be swept away from one
another once you are agreed that life is only life
forevermore together wing to wing and oar to oar.
Robert Frost

———————

Any intelligent woman who reads the marriage contract, and then goes into it, deserves all the consequences.
Isadora Duncan

If it were not for the presents, an elopement would be preferable.
George Ade

There is nothing nobler or more admirable than when two people who see eye-to-eye keep house as man and wife, confounding their enemies and delighting their friends.
Homer

There are six requisites in every happy marriage. The first is Faith and the remaining five are Confidence.
Elbert Hubbard

Marriage the happiest bond of love might be, if hands were only joined when hearts agree.
George Granville

---

*Behind every great man there is a surprised
woman.*
Maryon Pearson

———————

*It's a funny thing that when a man hasn't
anything on earth to worry about, he goes off
and gets married.*
Robert Frost

———————

*Marriage is popular because it combines the
maximum of temptation with the maximum of
opportunity.*
George Bernard Shaw

———————

*Marriage has many pains, but celibacy has no
pleasures.*
Samuel Johnson

———————

On second marriages
*Like the measles, love is most dangerous when it
comes late in life.*
Lord Byron

———————

The triumph of hope over experience.
Samuel Johnson

———————

We are number two. We try harder.
Avis Car Rental advertisement

When widows exclaim loudly against second marriages, I would always lay a wager that the man, if not the wedding day, is absolutely fixed on.
Henry Fielding

For I'm not so old, and not so plain. And I'm quite prepared to marry again.
W. S. Gilbert

I chose my wife, as she did her wedding gown, for qualities that would wear well.
Oliver Goldsmith

On husbands and wives

All husbands are alike, but they have different faces so you can tell them apart.
Ogden Nash

It is true that all married men have their own way, but the trouble is they don't all have their own way of having it!
Artemus Ward

Husbands are like fires. They go out if
unattended.
Zsa Zsa Gabor

_____

The best way to get husbands to do something is
to suggest that perhaps they are too old to do it.
Shirley MacLaine

_____

A husband's last words are always, 'OK, buy it!'
N. P. Willis

_____

If a husband has troubles, he should tell his
wife. If he hasn't, he should tell the world how
he does it.
N. P. Willis

_____

Husbands, love your wives, and be not bitter
against them.
The Bible

_____

Whoso findeth a wife, findeth a good thing.
The Bible

_____

An ideal wife is any woman who has an ideal
husband.
Booth Tarkington

_____

*When a woman gets married, it's like jumping
into a hole in the ice in the middle of winter.
You do it once and you remember it the
rest of your days.*
Maxim Gorky

---

*Every man who is high up likes to feel that he
has done it all himself. And the wife smiles and
lets it go at that. It's our only joke. Every
woman knows that.*
J. M. Barrie

---

*The man who says his wife can't take a joke
forgets that she took him.*
Oscar Wilde

---

*No man should have a secret from his wife.
She invariably finds it out.*
Oscar Wilde

On love

> To love someone deeply gives you strength.
> Being loved by someone deeply
> gives you courage.
> Lao Tzu

———————

> Love is best.
> Robert Browning

———————

> She rocks my world!
> David Beckham

———————

> If you have it [Love], you don't need to have
> anything else, and if you don't have it, it doesn't
> matter much what else you have.
> J. M. Barrie

———————

> Women are meant to be loved, not understood.
> Oscar Wilde

———————

> And all for love, and nothing for reward.
> Edmund Spenser

———————

> How do I love thee? Let me count the ways. I
> love thee to the depth and breadth and height
> my soul can reach.
> Elizabeth Barrett Browning

———————

Love is a friendship set to music.
E. Joseph Cossman

True love comes quietly, without banners or flashing lights. If you hear bells, get your ears checked.
Erich Segal

The best and most beautiful things in the world cannot be seen or even touched. They must be felt with the heart.
Helen Keller

Love is the triumph of imagination over intelligence.
Henry Louis Mencken

The course of true love never did run smooth.
William Shakespeare

At the touch of love everyone becomes a poet.
Plato

Love is more than gold or great riches.
John Lydgate

Love carries all before him. We too must yield to Love.
Virgil

———————

Love is a canvas furnished by Nature and embroidered by imagination.
Voltaire

———————

Love is like a precious plant. You can't just leave it in the cupboard or just think it's going to get on by itself. You've got to keep watering it. You've got to really look after it and nurture it.
John Lennon

———————

She who has never lov'd, has never liv'd.
John Gay

———————

Love is an irresistible desire to be irresistibly desired.
Robert Frost

———————

Love is a familiar. Love is a devil. There is no evil angel but Love.
William Shakespeare

———————

Various

> *Remember that happiness is a way of travel,*
> *not a destination.*
> Roy Goodman

I wish you health – a little wealth
And a happy home with freedom.
And may you always have true friends
But never have cause to need them.
Anon

> *Never argue at the dinner table, for the one*
> *who is not hungry always gets the best*
> *of the argument.*
> Richard Whately

Ninety per cent of the friction in daily life is
caused by the tone of voice.
Arnold Bennett

> *Whatever women do, they must do twice as well*
> *as men to be thought half as good. Luckily, this*
> *is not difficult.*
> Charlotte Whitton

The great question which I have never been able
to answer is, 'What does a woman want?'
Sigmund Freud

Women like silent men. They think they're listening.
Marcel Achard

A wise man makes more opportunities than he finds.
Francis Bacon

There are two times in a man's life when he should not speculate: when he can't afford it, and when he can.
Mark Twain

The most dangerous food a man can eat is wedding cake.
American proverb

There is nothing in the world like the devotion of a married woman. It's a thing no married man knows anything about.
Oscar Wilde

The only premarital thing girls don't do these days is cooking.
Omar Sharif

I often quote myself; it adds spice to my
conversation.
George Bernard Shaw

An optimist is a fellow who believes a housefly
is looking for a way to get out.
George Jean Nathan

Money won't buy happiness, but it will pay the
salaries of a large research staff to study the
problem.
Bill Vaughan

When a man sits with a pretty girl for an hour,
it seems like a minute. But let him sit on a hot
stove for a minute – and it's longer than any
hour. That's relativity.
Albert Einstein

Many a man in love with a dimple makes the
mistake of marrying the whole girl.
Stephen Leacock

My father gave me these hints on speechmaking:
be sincere, be brief, be seated.
James Roosevelt

If you don't strike oil in ten minutes,
stop boring.
Louis Nizer

———————

All women become like their mothers. That is
their tragedy. No man does. That's his.
Oscar Wilde

———————

Women have their faults,
Men have only two;
Everything they say,
Everything they do.
Anon

———————

She was a lovely girl. Our courtship was fast
and furious – I was fast and she was furious.
Max Kauffmann

———————

An honest man's the noblest work of God.
Alexander Pope

———————

Apologise to a man if you're wrong, but to a
woman even if you're right.
Anon

———————

An after-dinner speaker is a man who rises to the occasion and then stands too long.

Anon

Men are like fish; neither would get into trouble if they kept their mouths shut.

Anon

Blessed is the man who, having nothing to say, abstains from giving us wordy evidence of the fact.

George Eliot

Everything comes to him that hustles while he waits.

Thomas A. Edison

An old man gives good advice in order to console himself for no longer being in a condition to set a bad example.

La Rochefoucauld

Never go to bed mad. Stay up and fight.

Phyllis Diller

> *In matrimony, to hesitate is sometimes to*
> *be saved.*
> Samuel Butler

─────────────

Some less traditional toasts

Some speechmakers like to get away from the age-old toasts for good luck, health, happiness and may all your troubles be little ones. Here are a few examples of toasts that are less traditional. They could be particularly useful at small, informal wedding receptions where you don't want to sound pompous.

> 'To our friends. May Fortune be as generous with them as she has been in giving us such friends.'

─────────────

> 'To husbands – men when they are boys; boys when they are men; and lovable always.'

─────────────

> 'Long life and happiness – for your long life will be my happiness.'

─────────────

> 'To the bride and groom. May we all be invited to your golden wedding celebrations.'

─────────────

> 'To the bride. May she share everything with her husband, including the housework.'

─────────────

'To the bridegroom. He is leaving us for a better
life, but we are not leaving him.'

'May you live as long as you like, and have all
you like as long as you live.'

'To the lamp of true friendship. May it burn
brightest in our darkest hours and never flicker
in the winds of trial.'

'As Sydney Smith wrote: "Here's to marriage.
That happy estate that resembles a pair of
scissors, so joined that they cannot be separated,
often moving in opposite directions, yet
punishing anyone that comes between them."'

'Live today to the fullest! Remember, it's the first
day of the rest of your life.'

'To that nervous, fidgety, restless, impatient,
uncomfortable but enviable fellow, the groom.'

'To the bride. Let her remember that we give her
this husband on approval. He can be returned
for credit or exchange, but her love will not
be refunded.'

'Here's to your happy launching of the
Courtship on the Sea of Matrimony. May the
rocks be confined to the cradle!'

'To the happy bridesmaids, who today proved
the truth of Tennyson's sonnet: "A happy
bridesmaid makes a happy bride."'

'To the bride and groom. May the roof above you
never fall in and may you both never fall out.'

'To the bride and groom. As you slide down the
banister of life, may the splinters never face the
wrong way!'

'To the bride and groom. I wish you health, I
wish you happiness, I wish you wealth, I wish
you heaven – what more could I wish?'

Jokes and Anecdotes

Traditionally, a wedding reception was considered no place for comic stories, but times change and today jokes and funny anecdotes are quite acceptable, even expected, provided that they are of the kind that could be told to elderly relatives! What is important is that crude stories are avoided, as these embarrass people and spoil the occasion.

The best man's speech traditionally features jokes and it is vital that these are pitched correctly. Innocent jokes are suitable, but those that are malicious, blue or insulting must never be used. Making jokes at the expense of others is unforgivable, but making jokes at one's own expense is a good way of piquing and maintaining the attention of the audience. One-liners are often safer than long funny stories, which can fall flat if not cleverly told.

A suitable joke or humorous anecdote can do much to lighten a speech that would otherwise be all 'praise and thanks'. More than one – or two at the most – will make a fairly short speech seem like a comic routine – and, as we all know, some comedians' acts can go very flat indeed! You don't want the guests rolling in the aisles, and you don't want them grim with embarrassment or muttering, 'I really didn't understand that one!'

If you can adapt a joke to suit the situation, so much the better. But never include in your speech any joke or story that could possibly hurt or offend anyone present. Aim at raising a smile, not at raising a belly laugh, and do remember that it's the way you tell 'em that makes them successful. Lead into your joke naturally and keep it short, so neither you nor your audience loses track of it halfway through.

Here is a selection of jokes that you may find useful. Some, but not all, are about weddings and brides and grooms.

For the bride's father

A man inserted an ad in the classifieds: 'Wife wanted.' Next day he received a hundred letters. They all said the same thing: 'You can have mine.'

———————

Ian says he's a keen football fan and that he's an Arsenal supporter. I don't quite see the connection!

———————

When Helen was a small girl, she came home crying that a big girl had hit her. Her mother said, 'Which big girl? Did you hit her back?' 'Oh no,' said Helen. 'I hit her first!'

———————

A young couple on their wedding night were in their honeymoon suite. As they were undressing for bed, the husband, a big burly man, tossed his trousers to his new bride. He said, 'Here, put these on.' She put them on and the waist was twice the size of her body. 'I can't wear your trousers,' she said. 'That's right,' said the husband, 'and don't you ever forget it. I'm the one who wears the trousers in this family.' With that she flipped him her knickers and said, 'Try these on.' He tried them on and found he could only get them on as far as his kneecaps. 'Hey,' he said. 'I can't get into your panties!' She replied, 'That's right... and that's the way it is going to stay until your attitude changes!'

Things have changed. When we came home from work, we used to say, 'What's cooking?'
Nowadays, it's 'What's thawing?'

In Scotland, the most important time for a young lad is when he comes of age and is allowed to purchase and wear his first kilt. A couple of weeks before his important birthday, a young lad went to a tailor shop and found the material he wanted for his first kilt. He took the material to the tailor and said, 'I'd like ye to make me a kilt with this material here and, if ye don't mind, I'd like ye to make me a pair of matching underwear for it. I hear it gets a mite draughty up they things!' So the tailor took the material and promised to call the young lad when the order was completed. A few days later, the tailor called the lad back to the shop. 'Here's ye kilt, and here's ye matching underwear, and here's five yards of the material left over. Ye might want to take it home and keep it in case ye want anything else made of it.' So the lad rushed home with his order, threw the material in his room and donned his kilt. In his excitement, he decided to run to his girlfriend's house to show off his new purchase. Unfortunately, in his excitement, he forgot to don his underwear. When his girlfriend answered the door, he pointed to his kilt and said, 'Well, what'd ye think?' 'Ah, but that's a fine-looking kilt,' she exclaimed. 'Aye, and if ye like it, ye'll really like what's underneath,' he stated as he lifted his kilt to show her. 'Oh, but that's a dandy,' his girlfriend shouted admiringly. Still not realising that he didn't have his underwear on he exclaimed quite proudly, 'Aye, and if ye like it, I've got five more yards of it at home!'

Two men were sitting on the bank of a river, fishing. It was Sunday morning and the church bells were pealing in the nearby village. 'I feel a bit guilty,' said one. 'We shouldn't be here, we should have gone to church.' 'I don't feel guilty at all,' said the other. 'I couldn't have gone to church anyway. My wife's sick in bed.'

---

*The best way to remember your wife's birthday
is to forget it once.*

---

*Some people make the mistake of marrying for
better or worse but not for good.*

---

*We men never quite understand the phrase
'professional women'... Are there any amateurs?*

---

*The bride sobbed to her husband, 'Oh dear, I was
pressing your suit and the iron burnt a hole in
the trousers!' Husband comforted her. 'Now,
don't you worry. That suit has two pairs of
trousers.' 'Yes, I know,' said the wife, 'I used the
second pair to patch the hole!'*

---

*Adam: 'Eve, do you really love me?'
Eve: 'Who else?'*

---

*Someone once said that marriage is what
teaches a man frugality, regularity, temperance
– and other virtues he wouldn't have needed if
he'd stayed single.*

After the honeymoon, husband says to wife,
'You wouldn't mind if I pointed out a few of
your little defects, would you?' 'Not at all dear,'
she replied sweetly. 'It was those little defects
that stopped me from getting a better husband.'

———————

An estate agent was showing a woman around a
large house. 'I could do a lot with this,' she said.
Then added, 'On the other hand, I think that
was what I said the first time I saw my
husband.'

———————

For the groom

I'll never forget the day Julie told me I was
going to marry her...

———————

Matthew is a really tolerant person. He always
says, 'Be tolerant with those people who
disagree with you. They have a right to their
ridiculous opinions.'

———————

We were on a romantic weekend break in
Barcelona. As we sat outside after a wonderful
seafood meal with loads of wine out by the
marina, James gazed into my eyes and – in a
slightly slurred voice – said the immortal words:
'Monica, will you carry me?'

———————

The first time I dated Valerie, her father said she was just putting the finishing touches to her make-up, but she'd be down in a minute. Then he added, 'Care for a game of chess?'

———————

I've been told that a glass of champagne will cure all sorts of ills. All you need is a candle. You light the candle, drink the glass and wait five minutes. Then, drink another glass, still watching the candle. You keep this up until you can see three candles. Then, you blow out the middle one and go to sleep.

———————

Rob is a statistician. One day a young chap came up to him and said, 'Spare 50p mate, I haven't eaten for a week!' Rob got out his notebook. 'Really,' he replied. 'And how does that compare with the same period last year?'

———————

Today, I've been given two very useful pieces of advice. The first is: try praising your wife, even if it does frighten her at first. The second: if at first you don't succeed, do it the way your wife told you.

———————

My best man's trimmed his dangling locks, he's
cut and let them fall.
And all because of what he called, 'The cruellest
words of all.'
So now he's past the long hair stage. And
though I'm no contriver,
It did me good to hear him called, 'A crazy
woman driver.'

———————

The brain is a wonderful thing. It never stops
working from the time you are born until the
moment you start to make a speech.

———————

She: 'Can we get married soon?'
He: 'But, we won't be able to afford a home
for years!
She: 'We could live with your Mum and Dad!'
He: 'That just isn't possible. They're still living
with Dad's Mum and Dad.'

———————

It's funny how many women like a man with a
past. Of course, a man with a present is still
very popular.

———————

And so to my best man, Geoff. People have
asked me about Geoff's job. I say he's a visual
display technician. That's because he asked me
not to tell anyone that he's a window cleaner.

———————

Patrick, my best man, is a stout fellow. Well, stout, beer, ale, champagne...

For the best man

And so, without further ado, let me ask those of you who still can to stand up and join me in a toast...

Two middle-aged ladies were talking about marriage. 'I haven't seen my husband for 20 years,' said one. 'He went out to buy a cabbage, and never came back.' 'What on earth did you do?' asked the other. 'Oh, I just opened a tin of peas.'

Look how smartly turned out all the ushers are today. It's because they've all come straight from court...

Here is a wedding day weather forecast. Two warm fronts are converging, followed later by a little sun.

'Sorry, we've sold right out of geraniums in pots,' said the girl at the garden centre. 'What about some nice pots of chrysanths?' 'Oh, no,' said the customer. 'It was geraniums my wife told me to water while she was away.'

Many couples are unhappily married, but unfortunately they don't know it.

Husband: 'In our six years of marriage, we haven't been able to agree on a single thing!' Wife: 'No, it's been seven years, dear!'

Today's wedding is a love match, pure and simple. She's pure and he's simple.

Terry said he knew Debra could keep a secret. They'd been engaged for weeks before he knew anything about it!

Lisa and Ben are very independent people. I don't think they are as independent as one married couple I heard of, though. They sent individual Christmas cards! To the same people!

Nick, remember there's no place like home! Well,
after the other places close, anyway!

Somebody once said, 'No speech can be really
bad, if it's short enough.' Mine will be short!
Some of the best people hated making speeches.
Orville and Wilbur Wright, for example. Once, at
an important function, Wilbur was called upon
by the toastmaster. 'There must be a mistake,'
stammered Wilbur. 'Orville is the one who does
the speaking.' The toastmaster turned to Orville.
He rose and announced, 'Wilbur just made the
speech.'

Always remember, Gill and Peter, misfortune is
a point of view. No doubt, your headaches feel
good to an aspirin salesman!

There was this fellow who discovered a way to
hammer in nails without hitting his thumb. He
got his wife to hold the nail.

For the bride

A woman's work that is never done are the jobs she asked her husband to do.

Men are like computers... difficult to work out and never have enough memory.

It's often really hard for women to find men who are handsome, sensitive and caring... because so many of them already have boyfriends.

They say that bachelors like clever women because opposites attract.

I was advised to look out for a younger man – I might as well, they don't mature anyway!

Men are like coffee... the best ones are hot, rich and can keep you up all night long.

Men are like chocolate... smooth, sweet and they always head right for your hips.

They say the best thing to give a man who has everything... is a woman to show him how to work it.

_____

Unusual circumstances

Ladies and gentlemen, as you can see there are two best men. So why does it take two of us to describe the groom? Well, as the man in Moss Bros said, 'There's a lot to fit in.'

_____

At this point I'd like to congratulate the happy couple and say how happy I am they eventually got back together despite being apart for a short time. Linda always said that they'd get back together and, as Paul will testify, Linda is always right.

_____

They say, 'Never work with children or animals.' But I guess Anna wasn't listening. Today she becomes the official and much-loved stepmum to two children, a dog and a rabbit called Scary!

_____

For a small wedding reception

At small or informal wedding receptions, the speeches will generally be very short – in fact, little more than toasts. After the cake has been cut, the guests will probably circulate and chatter amongst themselves.

When this happens, there is always the risk of the happy atmosphere turning a little miserable; the conversation turning to hospitals and operations at one end of the room and to TV, sex and heavy drinking skills at the other. The bride may well be hissing, 'Somebody, do break up the cliques. Everybody should mix and be happy! Doesn't anyone know a funny story?' Here are a few, general, funny stories that might help to brighten things up and give the guests a chance to swap groups and circulate.

A mother and small daughter go into a police station. 'I want to report a missing person,' said the mother. 'Certainly madam,' replied the desk sergeant. 'Can you give me a brief description?' 'Well, he's over six foot tall, blond, blue-eyed and about 28 years old.' 'But Mummy, that doesn't sound anything like Daddy,' the small girl interrupted. 'You be quiet!' said her mother. 'We don't want him back.'

A man goes to Spain and attends a bullfight. Afterwards he goes to a nearby restaurant and orders the speciality of the day. The waiter brings him two very big balls on a huge plate, which the tourist eats with relish. The next day he goes to the same restaurant again, once again orders the speciality of the day, and he is brought two very big balls on a huge plate. It tastes even more scrumptious. The third day he does the same and the fourth, but on the fifth day he goes to the restaurant and orders the speciality of the day, and they bring him two very small balls on a big plate. The man asks, 'What gives?' and the waiter says, 'Senor, the bullfighter doesn't always win!'

The vicar's wife called round to welcome the newlyweds who had just moved into their new home in the village. As she rang the doorbell a large dog came up to her, wagging its tail happily. She was invited in and the dog accompanied her, settling itself alongside her on the brand new settee. After a chat and a cup of tea, she rose to leave – but to her horror, the dog jumped down, walked over to the standard lamp and solemnly lifted one leg. There was an extremely large puddle. Then the dog squatted. A large pile was added. The newlyweds smiled sweetly and completely ignored the dog's activities. The vicar's wife left rather hurriedly, and as she reached the garden gate she heard her name called. 'Excuse us, but you've forgotten your dog!' called the newlyweds.

A boy and his father were visiting a shopping centre in a country on their travels. They were amazed by almost everything they saw, but especially by two shiny silver walls that moved apart and back together again by themselves.

The lad asked, 'What is this, father?' The father, having never seen a lift, responded, 'I have no idea what it is.' While the boy and his father were watching wide-eyed, an old lady in a wheelchair rolled up to the moving walls and pressed a button. The walls opened and the lady rolled between them into a small room. The walls closed and the boy and his father watched as small circles lit up above the walls. The walls opened up again and a beautiful 24-year-old woman stepped out. The father looked at his son anxiously and said, 'Go get your mother.'

Tommy was late returning home from a friend's party and his parents were very worried. The phone rang. 'This is me, Tommy, the train broke down and we were put on a bus and I'm in a phone box and I don't know where I am!' 'I'll come and pick you up,' said Dad. 'On the wall under the mirror you'll see a card and on it will be the address of the phone box.' There was a very long pause. Then, 'Dad, I can't get the mirror off the wall!'

A customs officer, an MP, a vicar and a boy scout were aboard an aircraft that went out of control. The pilot ejected and there were only three parachutes to be found. The customs officer took one. 'I'm needed in the fight against smuggling,' he cried as he jumped. The member of parliament took the second. 'My constituents need me,' was his cry as he, too, leaped from the

plane. The vicar smiled at the young boy. 'I have
lived a good Christian life and I shall go to
heaven immediately. You take the last
parachute.' 'That's very good of you, sir,'
answered the boy scout. 'But we have a
parachute each. That customs officer took
my rucksack.'

The firm's boss was under stress. The business
was not doing at all well. His doctor
recommended a week's rest at a small nursing
home in the country. After a few days he was
much improved. However, the following week
the firm was phoned and told that, sadly, he had
suffered a relapse. 'What happened?' asked the
deputy boss. 'Well,' said the nursing sister, 'he
said he was a bit bored, so we suggested he
could help by sorting out the white from the
coloured items in the laundry room.' 'Oh my
goodness!' cried the deputy boss, 'you don't
mean you asked him to make decisions?'

'How old are you, Granny?' the small girl asked.
'I don't remember, dear,' said the grandmother.
'You could look in your knickers,' said the child,
helpfully. 'Mine say how old I am. Look! Four to
five years old!'

The group sat around the table, their fingers touching. 'Is there anybody there?' asked the medium. After a while, a cheery voice echoed round the room. 'Hi, Mary, this is me, George.' 'Goodness me,' cried one of the group. 'It's my late husband. How are you, dear? What's it like where you are?' 'Not too bad,' George's voice came back. 'The food's a bit boring though. Nothing but salads and more salads.' 'But do you feel loved, George?' asked Mary. 'Loved!' replied George. 'I don't know about loved, but there's more sex on offer than I can manage.' 'Oh dear, George,' cried Mary. 'Do you think you are in heaven or the other place?' 'Neither,' said George confidently. 'I'm a (expletive) rabbit!'

A man and a woman who have never met before find themselves in the same sleeping carriage of a train. After the initial embarrassment they both go to sleep, the woman on the top bunk, the man on the lower. In the middle of the night the woman leans over, wakes the man and says, 'I'm sorry to bother you, but I'm awfully cold and I was wondering if you could possibly get me another blanket.' The man leans out and, with a glint in his eye, says, 'I've got a better idea... just for tonight, let's pretend we're married.' The woman thinks for a moment. 'Why not,' she giggles. 'Great,' he replies. 'Get your own damn blanket!'

Bert was responsible for security on a huge building site. Fred was a happy-go-lucky labourer on the site. Bert always knew that Fred was helping himself to things that were not his, but he could never catch him. Every night Fred would push his barrow through the gate and every night Bert would stop him and make a thorough search. This went on for weeks, but Bert never found a stolen item. Many, many years after, the two met up by chance in a pub. 'Fred,' said Bert, 'I've retired now, but I've always wondered what you were up to on that building site. I know you were stealing something, but what?' Fred took a long swig from his glass. 'Wheelbarrows!' he said, triumphantly.

Stan was in court. 'You are the defendant, and you plead not guilty to stealing Farmer Brown's chickens. Is that correct?' asked the magistrate. 'I plead not guilty,' answered Stan, 'but I'm not the defendant. I'm only the chap who stole the chickens.'

When she was a very small girl, Emily was sitting on her mother's knee looking through a picture book of Bible stories. Before long they came to a drawing showing Christians being fed to the lions. Emily started to cry and her mother tried to calm her by telling her that the Christians would soon be with Jesus. Emily still wept. 'It's not fair,' she sobbed, 'that baby lion in the corner hasn't got a Christian!'

A woman who was delighted with the effect
some beauty treatment was having on her, wrote
to tell the beautician: 'Since my course of
treatment, I'm a different woman. My husband
is delighted!'

They had been married a year when the wife
confessed that she'd splashed out his money on
ten new pairs of shoes. 'Ten!' he exploded,
'What could you possibly want with ten new
pairs of shoes?' She smiled at him fondly, 'Ten
new handbags' she explained.

I heard someone in the wedding party
complaining about the suit he'd bought for the
wedding and saying that most sensible people
hired theirs. I said 'Think yourself lucky, they've
lowered mine!'

Did you see that drunk walking down the street
with one shoe on? A policeman said to him
'Did you lose a shoe?' The drunk said 'No.
I found one!'

When your daughter gets married and leaves
home, people say, to cheer you up, 'You're not
losing a daughter, you're gaining a son.' I'm
luckier than that, I'm also gaining a telephone!

I'm sure that we all know that women should have genuine equality these days and I'm the first one to agree that this is only fair. I only said so to my wife this morning as she was cleaning my car. Isn't that right, Jean?

Using props

Physical gags, games, visuals and tricks can also be part of a best man's speech. So if you don't want to be stuck just reading a prepared text – don't be. Let your imagination run wild and wow your audience with something different. If your speech is going to involve the use of props, make sure that you do plenty of rehearsal with them beforehand and also ensure that any machinery is in good working order before the big day.

Simple props can be used to begin with impact. A good idea for the best man, for example, could be to start off his speech with the remark: 'I hate it when people use cheap gimmicks to get attention, don't you?' before lifting up his trouser ends to reveal huge clown feet. Lots of different props can be used for this type of joke. Why not try a funny hat, a revolving bow tie, a whistle or a clown nose?

Alternatively, write a mock school report on the bride or groom and read it out, relating it to the events of the day, such as: 'It says here that Carrie doesn't suffer fools gladly... which is bad news as she's just got married to Alex.'

5 Rehearsing your Speech

Having written your speech, you are about halfway to becoming a successful speechmaker. You still have some work to do on your presentation though. Compare your situation, if you like, with that of an actor. An actor may know his lines perfectly, but he needs direction, rehearsal and self-discipline to make a success of the part he is to play.

How will you know your lines?

You could read from your script. This is certainly the easiest way for you to present your speech, but it's not good from the viewpoint of the guests at the wedding. They will expect to be spoken to, not read to. It will also sound unnatural and lack liveliness and spontaneity, and leave little or no opportunity for mentioning unexpected events of the day. It is these last-minute additions that can really bring a speech to life. Reading an entire speech from a sheet of paper will also stop you from making eye contact with the audience.

You could do as an actor does, that is, learn your speech by heart and then recite it. But are you a good enough actor to sound natural? Are you sure you won't forget your lines? And, if you have to make any last-minute changes to your speech, will you get confused?

Most speechmakers find that the best way of presenting a fairly short speech is to compromise between reading it and reciting it. This involves getting thoroughly familiar with the content, but learning by heart only the vital facts, such as names and how to pronounce them. To cut down on the amount of text you use, first write the speech out, then make very brief notes that remind you of each part of it. Gradually cut back on your text, so the notes say as much as you need to jog your memory.

Use prompts to remind you of what to say, such as a set of cue cards. These are small index cards with key phrases that remind you of different parts of your speech and are stacked in the order that you say them. Inserting blank cards for pauses can help you pace your speech. Even if you feel you need to put your whole speech on cards, they are still preferable to a piece of paper, because you will need to pause and look up as you turn them.

Now, read through your speech several times, first in your head, then out loud. Remember to pause at the places you have marked. After a while, you will find you are so familiar with the speech that you can look up from your script from time to time, and then refer to it again to bring you back on course.

Before long, you will need to refer to your script only occasionally. You will be sufficiently familiar with it.

Performance

By now, you should have a clear idea of the size of your audience and the size of the room in which the reception will be held. With a small number of guests in a small room, you'll be able to be heard speaking in your normal voice – unless you normally speak very quietly. If it is to be a large hall, with many guests, microphones may well be provided, so again, your normal voice will be fine. If there are no microphones, you will need to work on your volume, so that you reach those at the back, but without shouting.

Try a non-dress rehearsal, one day when you are alone. Stand behind a table with a chair behind you. Have a tumbler of water and a glass of wine in front of you. Prop a large mirror at the far side of the table. This will represent your audience, and will also show you what they will see.

Stand upright but relaxed. Nervous speakers often unconsciously clink loose change or keys in pockets, shuffle from one foot to the other, rock backwards and forwards, or fiddle with their hair or clothes. Try to avoid these or other distracting habits.

Perform your speech. Speak more slowly than you do normally, but not too slowly. Remember, the guests will be seated and you will be standing, so look out, as if over them with your head inclined slightly downwards. Smile now and then as you speak and let your gaze wander over all the guests. When you are referring to a particular person, turn your body – without shuffling your feet – so that you will be looking in the direction of that person. When you get to the toast, pick up your glass and drink the toast.

Now, be really critical of your performance, and see where it can be improved.

Did you wobble about – or, even worse, sway to and fro? Most inexperienced speechmakers do!

Were you able to hold your script easily? A piece of cardboard at the back would stop it flapping about. Or, you might prefer to write it out on a series of cards that you can hold in the palm of your hand. If you choose this method, make sure each card finishes at the end of a paragraph and do number the cards clearly, so that they cannot get out of order. A loose tag through the cards would make sure they stayed in order and that one was not dropped at a crucial time.

Did you wave your free arm about? An occasional gesture is fine; it prevents you from appearing wooden, but too much arm-waving will make you look more like a signalman than a speech-giver.

Delivery

The way a speech is delivered is very important. It is easy to sound pompous, but too much informality should also be avoided out of consideration for the importance of the occasion. You should by now know your speech quite well and you'll be aware of how you will look to your audience. You've got your voice level right for the room you'll be speaking in, so now you should check that your rate of speaking and your voice quality are satisfactory.

Practise your speech with the aid of the microphone supplied with most tape recorders and cassette players, setting the microphone well away from you if your voice will have to carry, without amplification, to the back of a large hall. Listen to your recorded speech and, again, be critical of yourself.

Better still, video your practice runs. Watch them critically and learn from them.

Perhaps you need to speak more slowly or more distinctly. Perhaps you should try to lower the pitch of your voice a little. Are you breathing properly? Take in a good breath at the beginning of each sentence and let it out easily as you speak. Never empty your lungs completely before taking another breath.

Are you concerned that you have an accent – local or foreign? Don't be! And don't try to 'talk posh' when it's not natural to you. However, don't be sloppy about pronunciation – especially of people's names, and do take a little care over your aitches and over words ending in d, t and -ing. You will then not only sound more professional, but also you'll be understood.

Summary of points to remember

Keep reminding yourself of these important points as you work through your planning and practice. Plus, there's one other important rule if you feel things are not working as well as they should: it's the KISS principle, meaning 'keep it simple, stupid'.

Do...

- Plan your speech thoroughly;
- Write bold headlines on small cards organised in small sections, and number the pages;
- Rehearse your speech until you are very comfortable with the words and your delivery;
- Dress unobtrusively, and avoid anything that jangles or will be distracting;
- Stand still, comfortably relaxed and upright, with feet slightly apart;
- Speak clearly but not so loudly that you could shatter a pane of glass at ten paces;
- Hold your cards in your hand or hold your hands behind your back;
- Take a deep relaxing breath before beginning, and remember to breathe throughout the speech;

- Be flexible if you have something amusing to add;
- Look at the audience as you speak, but don't fix them with a stare;
- Speak slowly and clearly, varying your speed and voice levels;
- Keep the tone conversational;
- Remember that the audience is not critical – they are there to enjoy themselves, to eat, talk and congratulate the bride and groom;
- Be brief – three minutes is ample, five minutes is maximum and six minutes is too long. Consider how *you* feel about speeches made at a social function;
- Be appropriate, to the point and sincere;
- Limit the number of drinks before your speech.

Don't...

- Clink loose change in your pocket;
- Shuffle your feet;
- Ease your tie away from your collar – you are not on trial for your life;
- Mop your face with a handkerchief;
- Compete with noise, but *do* wait for silence;
- Say 'Unaccustomed as I am to public speaking...';
- Use unnecessarily long words or sentences;
- Use formal words or unusual phrases;
- Swear, use slang, tell lies, be pompous or patronising;

- Tell embarrassing stories or mention anything sensitive;
- Tell jokes that make fun of anyone but yourself;
- Forget to respond to and propose the toast;
- Forget to have a glass of water at hand.

Best man — introduction of speakers

If you are the best man, you will know whether there is to be a professional toastmaster at the reception or if it will fall to you to introduce those making the speeches. If the task falls to you, now is the time for you to try out your statements of introduction.

Yours will be the first voice the guests hear as they sit, replete, awaiting the speeches. You must command attention and your few words must be understood. Practise standing up straight, smiling pleasantly and saying very clearly: 'Ladies and gentlemen – the father of the bride'; or: 'Ladies and gentlemen – Mr John Brown will now propose a toast to the bride and groom', where the bride's father is not proposing the toast.

Your second introduction can be equally simple. 'Ladies and gentlemen – the groom' or 'Ladies and gentlemen – the groom will now reply to the toast' will be sufficient.

How you introduce yourself will need to be discussed with the bridegroom. He may wish to introduce you at the end of his speech, especially if he has proposed the toast to the bridesmaids early in his speech or if there are no bridesmaids. He will end by saying something like: 'And now it's the turn of Sam, my best man, to say a few words to you.' If you have to introduce yourself, all you need say is: 'Ladies and gentlemen – I expect you've realised by now that I am the best man,' and then give your own speech.

If the bride wishes to speak, introduce her after you have read any messages with something very encouraging, like: 'I'm sure you'll be delighted that the bride is now going to say a few words to us all. Ladies and gentlemen – the bride.'

So, along with practising the performance and delivery of your speech, do give some attention to the performance and delivery of your introductions. It is a simple task, but it needs doing well.

Dress rehearsal

About a week before the wedding, arrange a dress rehearsal. Put on a good suit and set out the table, chair and glasses as before. If you have or can borrow a flash camera and a video camera, these will be very useful, since at many modern weddings, the speeches are punctuated with flashes from amateur photographers and the panning and zooming of video buffs.

Invite your wife, partner or a friend whose opinion you trust to be your audience of one. Tell them that your speech is in its final state and that, unless you have made any dreadful errors, it will not be changed. Ask them to video you as you deliver your speech and occasionally to take a flash photograph – or at least make the camera flash occasionally.

Reassure them that you are not seeking a professional film of your dress rehearsal, but just atmosphere. What you do need is a valued opinion on your performance of the speech. Above all, can you be heard and understood; but also, have you any irritating habits that you are unaware of, but that might annoy the wedding guests? We all have such involuntary habits as needlessly pushing up spectacles, rubbing the nose or brushing back the hair. You must do your utmost to keep these under strict control for the time of your speech.

Hopefully, your valued audience of one will applaud your speech, or at least say, 'Well, I've heard a lot worse!' And, of course, you can always view the video film he or she took to confirm the opinion.

Now, you will have reaped the benefit of your efforts. You will feel more self-confident. You will feel sure that you have prepared a good speech and that you will present it competently.

Delivery

There are three important things to remember on the big day. The first is vital! Before you leave for the wedding, and again at the reception, check that you have the script of your speech with you. The second is more advisory. Don't imbibe too much prior to making your speech. You may think an extra glass of wine will relax you, but the chances are that instead it will make you woolly-headed. The third is for your own comfort and wellbeing. Even if you don't feel the need, visit the toilet about ten minutes before the speeches are due to start.

The preliminaries...

If there is a toastmaster, he or she will make sure the guests' glasses are filled, the microphones – if such there are – are well placed and working, and the speechmakers are in place and ready. He will then call for the guests' attention and announce the first speechmaker.

Where there are no microphones, it is a good idea if those organising the wedding ask a reliable guest – perhaps an usher – to stand at the back of the room to signal to the speakers that their voices are reaching all. This will avoid the unprofessional 'Can you hear me at the back?' 'No!' routine, which can be distracting to guests and speaker alike.

Those guests with video cameras should have been asked to stay in their seats during the speeches, so as not to distract the speechmakers or obstruct the guests' view.

Just in case there are badly behaved children or noisy elements among the guests, it would be advisable to ask a few friends to stand by so that they can deal gently and politely with potential problem areas early on.

When there is no toastmaster, the job of gaining the attention of the guests and announcing the speakers normally falls to the best man. If you are the best man, you will know what is expected of you and will be poised to introduce the opening speaker at the appropriate time.

The guests, having had their glasses filled, will be anticipating the speeches, so a light tap on a tumbler, and a call for attention – with a friendly smile – should do the trick. Then, making sure that the opening speechmaker is ready for action, you can make the introduction.

...and 'Action!'

Now to you, the speechmaker. Before you rise to make your speech, check where anyone to whom you'll be referring is seated – so that you can look in their direction at the appropriate moment. Know where your handkerchief is – in case you need it – and make sure your water tumbler and wine glass are to hand, but not in danger of being knocked over.

When your big moment arrives, tell yourself how calm and well prepared you are. Stand, then pause for an instant, remembering to smile as you gaze over the guests. They will smile back, encouragingly, and you can begin to address them.

Remember: you are not racing against the clock. If a joke in your speech causes a laugh or a murmur, be happy that your audience is with you, and wait, smiling, for quiet before proceeding.

For the time that you are delivering your speech, you are in charge. If you should be so unfortunate as to be faced with an ill-mannered guest who interrupts you, wait for him or her to be silent – or to be politely silenced by others – and then carry on without comment. Should you find you've made a mistake, smile and say 'Sorry!' – but without becoming flustered. Then correct your error.

Then, it will be all over and you'll be sitting down to the smiles of appreciation and the applause. Was it worth all the preparation? Of course it was! You were a successful speechmaker! Congratulations!

Perfect delivery

Remember these points to ensure your speech goes with a bang.

- Take your time. Leave time for the audience to react and to applaud or laugh in places.

- Stand tall and maintain eye contact with members of the audience. Looking at familiar faces might help to calm your nerves.

- Allow for interruptions. Don't get panicked and start speaking over them. They can provide thinking time and will get the audience involved.

- Remember that the audience is on your side and that you are among friends. This is not an exam, so relax and enjoy it.

Specimen Traditional Speeches

Having acquired as much information as you can about the wedding and all who are involved, you have started preparing your speech. But even with all your research and information you may still be finding it difficult to put pen to paper. If you are really stuck, all you have to do is to select a specimen speech from this chapter or from Chapter 8 (pages 101–124) – the speech that seems most suitable for the occasion – and change the names and facts appropriately. Even if you prefer to write your own speech, you may find some material you wish to use here.

Toast to the bride and bridegroom

This is proposed by the bride's father.

Specimen 1

'Hello, for those of you who don't know me, I am Jack, Laura's dad. On behalf of my wife Jean and I, I would like to give a warm welcome to all the relatives and friends who have joined us to celebrate Laura and Geoff's marriage. I know that some of you have travelled long distances to be here. Thank you all for coming to help celebrate this very special day.

'As I look around the room, I realise how many friends Laura and Geoff have, and I hope that you all had a wonderful afternoon and that you will have a great evening. I'd also like to take this opportunity to thank everyone else involved in making the day so special, including Jean and Anna for their efforts with the wedding invitations and order of service. Not to mention the staff here at Ludwell Hall for this superb reception.

'Today, I must admit that I am the proudest dad in the world to have accompanied Laura down the aisle. I think that you will all agree that she looks absolutely stunning. My wife and I are both very proud of how she looks today, and how she has grown up... and are both delighted that she has found someone who she obviously loves and cares so much for.

'Since Laura was a little girl we have been saving for her wedding. However, after some of the drips she brought home we gradually started dipping into the money and then the wedding fund actually became known as the BMW! However, when we met Geoff we knew she was on to a winner – despite him unfortunately supporting Everton, a

Vancouver Public Library
Checkout Receipt

Firehall Branch Library
Date (MM/DD/YY): 08/18/17 03:07PM
****

How to write wedding speeches & toasts /
Item: 31383093487372
Call No.: 808.55 J46h
Due Date (MM/DD/YY): 09/08/17

Total: 1

Item(s) listed due by closing
on date shown.

For renewals, due dates, holds, fines
check your account at www.vpl.ca
or call Telemessaging at 604-257-3830

Access VPL anywhere, any time and
on-the-go! Stream or download audiobooks,
magazines, movies, music and more via
your digital library. Free with your
VPL card at vpl.ca/DigitaLibrary

Please retain this receipt

fact we have decided to overlook – and the wedding account was up and running again. And lucky, too, because no sooner had Geoff been coming round a few times for tea when he did the deed and proposed.

'Anyway we are thrilled to bits to have him as a son-in-law and feel like he is already part of the family. While Laura and Geoff are celebrating this union, don't think they are alone. Jean and I have been trying to sell off Laura for years, but with little success. Today we got desperate enough to give her away!

'We just have a few words of wisdom for the pair to remember, based on my 35 years of married life; Laura – If you want something from Geoff, just ask for it. Don't forget he's a man and hints don't work. Geoff – When you're getting ready to go out, remember, "No, Laura, your bum doesn't look big in that."

'But seriously, Aristotle once said, "Love is composed of a single soul inhabiting two bodies." May Laura and Geoff be blessed with happiness that grows... and with love that lasts... and a peaceful life together.

'I wish them enjoyment for today, the fulfilment of all their hopes and dreams for tomorrow and love and happiness, always.

'It is now my pleasure to propose a toast to the happy couple. Ladies and gentlemen, please be upstanding and raise your glasses, I give you... the bride and groom, the new Mr and Mrs West.'

Specimen 2

'Ladies and gentlemen, I'm afraid I am not much of an orator. In fact, I think the last speech I made in public was at my own wedding. Now, how long ago was that? One grows so forgetful as one grows older.

'We are so pleased to welcome you all here today and we feel sure that none of us will ever forget what a perfect picture Jane and Stephen made as they stood together in church. Mind you, Jane was so late starting out that I began to wonder if you'd all have turned up for nothing. But she made it in the end. Ah, well, it is the bride's privilege. She told me the reason she was so late was that she couldn't get her veil right.

'You all saw that she got it right in the end – and everything else as well. I dare say Stephen didn't mind waiting for a girl who arrived looking such a picture.

'In any case, I am sure they have such a long and happy future stretching before them that a few minutes here or there makes little difference. It doesn't matter so much, after all, if you are married at two o'clock or ten past two – so long as you are married to the right partner. And I have never been so sure of anything in my life as that these two have done just that – found the right partner.

'People always say at weddings something like, "I hope their married life will be as happy as my own." I'll add to that; I'll say I hope their married life will be as happy as my wife has made my own. For it's a good wife that makes a good marriage – and that's just what Stephen has managed to find.

'So, ladies and gentlemen – friends – I ask you to rise and lift your glasses, as we drink a toast of long life and great happiness to the bride and groom. [Pause] *To Jane and Stephen!*'

Specimen 3

'Good afternoon everyone, I am Mike, the bride's father. Twenty-five years ago Kerry was born, I blinked and here I am, giving the father of the bride speech. Where has the time gone?

'Cerys and I would sincerely like to welcome [insert people to be thanked here]. It is lovely to see so many of you turn up for Kerry and Tim's special day.

'We are so proud today to see Kerry looking so beautiful. She has been full of life throughout the years she lived at home. She has always brightened up our lives... by never turning off the lights. She says she has nothing to wear... but manage to fill five wardrobes with it. Seriously though, she is very special to us.

'We are also very proud that she has married Tim, a very special young man.

We could not have had a nicer young man joining the family and on their behalf I bid him a warm welcome. He has not had an opportunity to meet most of them and only distance keeps them away today. Time, however, will rectify this, and he will be welcomed by them all.

'Handing Kerry over to Tim reminds me of what my own father-in-law, Geoff, said at our wedding:

If you love something, set it free.

If it comes back, it was, and always will be, yours.

If it never returns, it was never yours to begin with.

And if all it does is just sit in your house, mess up your stuff, spend your money, eat your food, use the telephone all night and monopolise your TV...

You either married it or gave birth to it!

'Ladies and gentlemen, please be upstanding. I would like to propose a toast... to the bride and groom.

'I would now like to hand you over to my son-in-law, Tim.'

Specimen 4

'We are all here to be present at the happy occasion of the marriage of my daughter Honey and Jake, and to wish them well in their life together. They will make an excellent couple and together I am sure that they will prosper.

'Sylvia and I will miss her. She has been my bobby-dazzler and always will be, but Jake and Honey must lead their own lives. They have their sights set on what they wish to achieve in their life together and I am sure that they will achieve it.

'I bring with me best wishes from all the family, from each and everyone, and also all those friends that know Honey, to the happy couple.

'Now it is with great pride and pleasure that I ask you to rise and drink the health of my treasured daughter Honey and of Jake and to wish them a long and very happy life together.'

Tip

Wait for all of the glasses to be filled before asking guests to stand for the first toast.

Bridegroom's reply

This includes the toast to the bridesmaids or matron of honour.

Specimen 1

'Thank you, Bob, for that wonderful speech. I was quite confident earlier but now I am not sure how I am going to top that! My wife and I [pause for cheers] would like to thank both sets of parents for all their help with today. 'Thanks, too, to the ushers and my best man. When I first set the wedding day I instantly knew who I wanted to be my best man but unfortunately he couldn't make it so I settled for Matt instead! I would also like to mention how beautiful the bridesmaids look, although I'm sure you will all agree that my new bride is the most beautiful of all. Before I continue I would like to show my appreciation for people, so if I can get all the bridesmaids and ushers, best man and parents to come up we would like to give you all a gift to show you our gratitude. [Give out gifts]

'As you can all agree, my new wife looks absolutely fantastic. Sally, you took my breath away when I saw you coming down the aisle. I knew Sally was the one for me when we had our first big argument. I thought that anyone who could stand up to me and still look so lovely had to be my wife.

'It says everything about Sally and why I love her so much that she's put so much effort into making the day special and enjoyable not just for the two of us, but also for everyone here today. In planning the wedding, Sally will have spoken to me at some point about each and every person in the room here and how you will enjoy the day. She is the most thoughtful and kind person I have ever met and that is why I love you so much.

'I'd like to finish with a quote from Robert Browning that's worth thinking about: "Grow old along with me, the best is yet to be." Sally, I can't wait to grow old with you and I look forward to experiencing the best of life with you. Please raise a glass to my wife, Sally Deng.'

Specimen 2

'Ladies and gentlemen, Jane and I want to thank you, Andrew, for those kind words and good wishes. Needless to say, we are both delighted to be here today!

'Sarah – I must now think of her as mother-in-law – has worked so hard making all the arrangements for our big day. And Andrew – father-in-law! – has, so he tells us, considered taking out a second mortgage as Sarah got on with the planning. Jane and I are so grateful to them, not only for this wonderful reception, but also for letting us share their home until we can set up our own. Our sincerest thanks!

'And I must thank my own parents for all they have done for me over the past twenty-mumble years. They have been marvellous... No, Mum made me promise that I wouldn't tell you my age. She said it would make her seem old! Looking at her today, you'll all agree she could have been scarcely three years old when she had me!

'I'm sure you'll all agree that I am the luckiest man in the world. I have wonderful parents and parents-in-law. I have a beautiful, intelligent and hard-working wife. Actually, she has a long list of qualities – but I can't decipher her handwriting...! And I have such marvellous friends and relations, here to share the day with us. My wife and I want to thank you all for coming to our wedding, and for your very generous presents. Thank you!

'We are both particularly pleased to see Jane's cousin, Polly, who flew in from Vancouver only yesterday, and Uncle John, who made the long journey down from Newcastle especially to be with us. And, I'm sure, we are all thinking with affection of those who aren't able to be here today.

'I see, out of the corner of my eye, that Peter, my best man, is getting impatient, waiting to make his speech. So far, he's been a perfect best man, I'm sure you'll all agree. I say "so far" because we haven't heard his speech yet!

'You see, he did tell me a rather ominous best man story. This best man was asked to include in his speech verse 18, chapter 4, of the First Epistle of John, which reads: "There is no fear in love; but perfect love casteth out fear." Unfortunately, he read, instead, from the Gospel according to St. John, and came up with, "For thou hast had five husbands; and he whom thou now hast is not thy husband." After that story, I thought it safer to leave the content of Peter's speech entirely up to him!

'However, he does have the duty of replying to my toast to the matron of honour. Jenny has been absolutely marvellous. Not only does she look wonderful, but she has given wonderful support to Jane, both today and throughout all the preparations.

'So, ladies and gentlemen, please stand and lift your glasses and join me in this toast to the matron of honour. [Pause] To Jenny!'

Specimen 3

'Thanks very much, Fred, for that witty speech. Hello, everyone, and thank you very much for coming. I will attempt to keep this quite short so that you can all get back to the drinking.

'Firstly, I would like to start off by saying how lucky I am. Katrina's a beautiful girl with a heart of gold, and she deserves a good husband... Thank God I married her before she found one!

'Only joking... Katrina I know that I told you earlier, but I want everyone to know how beautiful you look today. Your dress is stunning and you really do look like a princess. You really have made me the happiest and proudest man alive today by saying "I will" and I can't wait to tell everyone that you are now Mrs Atkins, at every opportunity. As Katrina will tell you, I'm often wrong – but in marrying her, I know I've made the right decision. Thank you, darling.

'My thanks go out to everyone who helped with the preparations for today, I'm sure you will all agree how fantastic the wedding was and the reception looks amazing. We have some gifts for everyone, which we will hand out afterwards so that we can continue with the speeches.

'Before I ramble on too much I will stop now and all that remains is to propose a toast... to the new Mrs Katrina Atkins!'

Best man's reply

This is made on behalf of the bridesmaids or matron of honour.

Specimen 1

'Hi, good afternoon, ladies and gentlemen. For those of you
who don't know me my name is Luke and I'm Frank's best
man. Well, I'm the best he could get, or at least I'm the
only guy who would agree to do it!

'Firstly, I would like to welcome you to this special
celebration of Frank and Louise's marriage. Now before I
hand you over to the father of the bride I would just like to
say a big thank you to the bridesmaids [insert names],
flower girls [insert names] and page boy [insert name],
because they have all done a marvellous job in helping
Louise, and look fantastic. Indeed, they are only eclipsed by
Louise herself, who, I'm sure you'll all agree, looks
absolutely stunning today. Frank, on the other hand, just
looks stunned.

'I'm very happy that Frank has found the woman of his
dreams. As a wise person once said, "Love is grand."
However, keep in mind, Frank, that divorce is a hundred
grand!

'The marriage ceremony asks that couples take each other
for better or for worse. Well, Frank, in finding Louise you
really couldn't have done any better. Louise – you couldn't
have done any worse.

'Of course, it's also traditional for the best man to tell a
witty anecdote about the groom, something that gives an
insight into his character. Unfortunately with Frank, when
we sat down to think about it we discovered nothing funny
had ever happened to him. As with most best man/groom

relationships there are the stories I'm not allowed to tell, like the time we both ended up stranded in France without any money after a lad's weekend away. However, if you see me at the bar later I may be persuaded to reveal all.

'Joking aside now, Frank's been a great friend to me and we've had some excellent times together. I'm sure we'll have more in the future and it's been an honour to be the best man today. When Frank told me he had asked Louise to marry him, I was obviously delighted and I wish them all the happiness in the world.

'Ladies and gentlemen, for those of you that are still capable of standing, would you now do me the honour of rising to your feet... and raising your glasses to the newlyweds. Here is to love and laughter and happiness ever after. I give you the bride and groom, Frank and Louise.'

Specimen 2

'Ladies and gentlemen, on behalf of the bridesmaids, I should like to thank Sam for his toast, and I must say that I'm really enjoying myself – the opportunity of being surrounded by a gathering of pretty women doesn't happen every day. It's a pity we're only allowed one bride – I'd marry them all if I could – and if they'd have me!

'A lot has been said about the bride today, and I would like to say some more! She looks absolutely gorgeous and she's a fabulous person, too. Sam's a very lucky guy – he's looking so smug and pleased with himself that he doesn't really need any congratulations.

'Perhaps some of you don't know how all this started. Well – Sam was at a party and he tried to phone me to ask where I'd got to. Instead of me he got a wrong number.

Tracey was on the other end and after a long conversation he asked her for a date. Need I say more? – except that I wish it was me who'd made that phone call – I've never had such good fortune!

'Sam may not think he needs any congratulations, but I'm going to wish them both all the luck in the world anyway, and I'm sure that everyone will agree that this has been a great wedding.'

Specimen 3

'Good evening, ladies and gentlemen. For those of you who don't know me, I'm Sean, Joe's younger brother. It's great to be standing up here today because, after all these years, Joe has finally admitted that I am the best man.

'No, seriously, it's the first time I've been asked to be a best man, it's the first time I've ever been here to the Swallow Hotel, it's the first time that Joe has complimented me in over 25 years, but best of all it's the first time Joe's ever paid for dinner.

'Well I can honestly say in Miranda he has managed to get one of the best girls possible. I do have to say how lucky you are Joe. You will leave here today having gained a wife who is warm, loving and caring, who is both funny, and beautiful. And Miranda, you'll leave here today having gained – a gorgeous dress and a lovely bouquet of flowers.

'Well, I won't keep you any longer. I know Joe's dying to buy you all a drink at the bar. It just remains for me to say what an honour it was today to be standing here as Joe's best man and see Joe walk Miranda down the aisle.

'It now it gives me immense pleasure, not to mention relief, to invite you all to stand and raise your glasses in a toast... to the new Mr and Mrs Lydon. We wish them well for the future and hope they enjoy a long, happy marriage.'

Specimen 4

'Ladies and gentlemen, I am called the best man, but goodness knows why, because no one pays much attention to a man in my position today. They all say, "Isn't the bride radiant?" and "Doesn't the groom look dashing?" and "How pretty the bridesmaids are!" But you never hear anyone say, "What a fine figure of a man the best man is!" If they notice me at all they think I'm one of the caterers!

'But enough about me. I am standing up at the moment to speak for the bridesmaids, to say thank you on their behalf for the kind things Phil said about them. To tell you the truth I don't think he did them justice, but then that's understandable on a day like this. I'm surprised he even noticed that they were there at all, the way he's been looking at Tracey. Never mind, I'm still a bachelor and my judgement is emotionally unclouded, and I think they're the finest looking set of bridesmaids I've ever seen. I can see that you all agree with me. So on behalf of the bridesmaids, thank you very much indeed.'

Tip

Stay away from crude and smutty material. You do not want to offend or embarrass anyone.

At the end of the best man's speech, it is usual for him to read out the names of those who have sent congratulatory messages, giving the actual greetings (after editing any that are of too risqué a nature!) from several of these. He should check first with the bride and bridegroom if there are any they specifically want included. The remainder are left displayed for the guests to see later.

If the bride wishes to speak, the best man should introduce her, briefly, if there is no toastmaster at the reception.

Following her speech (or immediately after the messages, if she is not speaking), the best man should advise the guests what is happening next in the programme. He may also be asked to tell them the plans for the remainder of the celebrations.

Bride's speech

There is no need for the bride to say anything at all at the wedding reception. In fact, traditional wedding etiquette provides no place for a speech from her.

However, bride's speeches are becoming more popular nowadays. What began as the bride's friends insisting on an impromptu speech is nowadays anticipated with some speech preparation by the bride – just in case. Or, the bride may particularly wish to say a few words.

The ideal place for the bride's speech would be immediately after her husband has replied to the toast to the two of them. But following on immediately from the toast to the bridesmaids, her speech, especially if she proposes a toast, will be out of place. It is more appropriate then, for the bride's speech to be the last one, just after the best man's reply.

Generally, the bride's speech is short – a few sentences will be adequate – although this is also changing at some weddings.

Specimen 1

'I thought it only right that I start married life as I mean to go on – by having the last word!

'Those of you who know me, probably aren't surprised that I want to say a few words today. Those of you who know me really well, will be surprised if it is only a few words!

'The main reason I wanted to speak today was to personally say thank you to some very special people who have contributed to today. [Insert names of people to be thanked here]

'I'd also like to thank Ian for his earlier compliments and would like to add how wonderful he looks today. You have been my rock and I am so proud to be standing here today as your wife. I won't say any more as I know I'll start to cry!

'So all it leaves is for me to thank everyone for coming. I know you all want to get back to your champagne so I'll leave you to it, but thanks so much for being here and making our day so special. I'd like to propose a toast to you guys, who have made it such a special day for us – to family and friends, to the guests!'

Specimen 2

'Ladies and gentlemen, our families and all of my friends, it is very kind of you to insist that I break with tradition and speak to you all. I'm very pleased to have the opportunity, actually, of joining my thanks to those of my husband, for your help, support and your wonderful gifts to us.

'I'm not going to say very much, except that life is full of surprises and that Stephen is the best surprise that's ever happened to me.

'To see so many friends here, along with the best mums and dads in the world, our wonderful godparents and all of our relatives, makes our day absolutely perfect. Thank you all very much indeed.'

Specimen 3

'Friends and family, I'd like to thank all of you for being here today, especially since many of you knew that I'd want to say a few words... it's very touching that you still decided to come.

'Firstly, I would like to thank my bridesmaids. You have all done a magnificent job and have helped me a lot today. Secondly, my parents; you have done more to help me than I can thank you for. But I'll try. Thank you.

'From the moment Lewis and I got engaged I've been thinking about this wedding. I just wanted everything to be perfect and was determined not to overlook even the most insignificant detail. But I needn't have worried, his best man made sure he was there.

'I'm so glad to be married to Lewis. Caring, talented, modest, charming – I can see why he picked me. Seriously, I don't think there could ever be anyone in this world more perfect for me than Lewis is and I appreciate my good fortune in marrying such a warm-hearted and loving man. When we first started going out together I was attracted by his ambition, drive and determination. Three years later, when he proposed to me, I realised that without those qualities our marriage would still be as strong and I'd love him just as much. Lewis brings out the good in me, he makes me laugh and he makes me enjoy each and every moment of life just by being a part of mine. They say that you don't marry someone you can live with – you marry the *person who you cannot live without. This is certainly true with Lewis. I simply couldn't live without him and I look forward to growing old and grey with him at my side.*

'There isn't much more for me to say than thank you to everybody who has helped today go so fantastically. Thank you all.'

Specimen 4

'After six years together I expect many of you were wondering if we would ever get round to getting married – I know I was.

'Well it may have taken us a while but I'm delighted to be able to finally stand here as Mark's wife. Today would not have gone nearly so well without the generous help of so many people – and whilst my husband has already taken care of the thank-yous, I would like to single out a few of you for my own praise. [Insert details of people whom you wish to thank]

'Let me end as I began, by thanking you all once again for coming tonight. I can honestly say that today would not have been the same if we had not been in the company of our dear friends and family. At weddings it is the guests that create the party atmosphere and you good people have certainly done that for us. May I propose a toast to love, laughter and friendship.

'Cheers!'

Specimen Unconventional Speeches

The basis of a traditional wedding speech is pretty much governed by convention, but in certain situations the guidelines may need a little modification to fit the occasion.

Pregnancy

If the bride is obviously pregnant and blooming, you may wish to acknowledge this in the speeches or perhaps you want to use this as an opportunity to let people know the happy news. Needless to say, it's best to confirm this with the couple before blurting out the news to everyone. And, despite what you may wish to say, jokes about shotgun weddings or how 'I bet you all thought the bride was just fat' will definitely not be appreciated.

By the father of the bride

Specimen 1

'As those of you with good eyesight will know, Caroline is expecting. And did anyone ever see a more beautiful, blooming bride walk up the aisle? I speak for all my family when I say how proud we are of her.'

Specimen 2

'When Janine told us she was getting married to Ben, my wife and I couldn't have been more delighted. We rushed out to buy champagne and celebrate. A month later they were back for Sunday lunch saying they had something serious to tell us. We held our breath for a minute, I can tell you. Was the wedding off, we wondered? What on earth did they want to tell us? Well, ladies and gentleman, I can now tell you. Janine is expecting our first grandchild and we couldn't be happier for them. So please be upstanding and drink a toast to Janine, Ben and the bump!'

By the groom

Specimen 1

'Some of you may have noticed that Emma has not had a drink today. A shock, I know, to anyone who knows her! Well we are pleased to tell you that that is because she is pregnant! The baby is due in November and we couldn't be happier. So please raise your glasses of champagne – orange juice for Emma – in celebration.'

Specimen 2

'For years, ladies and gentleman, friends and family have told me that it really was time for me to settle down. And for years, I have completely ignored them. But being with Karen has made me stop and think about my priorities in life. I know now that I want my life to be centred around her and our family. And, yes, it's already started – we're expecting our first child next April...'

By the bride

Specimen 1

'When Adrian and I decided to get married, it was because we realised that the time had come to cement our relationship and start work on making a family together. When he proposed and I accepted, "overjoyed" is not an adequate description of how we both felt. So much so, in fact, that our celebrations have resulted in our plans being brought forward quite substantially. So everyone please mark 18th February in your diaries now, as that is the date that we are expecting our first baby!'

By the best man

Specimen 1

'Kelly and Andy have never been a couple to do things by halves. Having met at university and got engaged before they even had their degrees, it was a bit much to expect them to wait until the honeymoon to start their family. I am delighted that the pair are expecting their first child together. Congratulations!'

Specimen 2

'Biology was never Johnny's best subject when we were at school. So when he and Lisa told me they were expecting, it came as something of a surprise that Johnny had finally worked out what to do. Several orange juices later (yes, they've given up alcohol together!), the mystery was solved – it turns out Lisa took A-level biology.'

By the chief bridesmaid

Specimen 1

'Whilst I expected to stand up here and give a speech as the chief bridesmaid, I didn't expect to be addressing you as an auntie. Yes, my little sister and her new husband have given me permission to give you the fantastic news that they are expecting!'

Specimen 2

'On my first day at school, my mum dropped me at the door and told me I had to be brave and not to cry – I lasted about a minute before the tears started. Then suddenly, an arm was put around me and someone started telling me it would be all right. Sophie had arrived in my life. Frankly, she's been mothering me ever since! But as we all know, Sophie will soon have someone else to mother. I'm sure she'll make the very best mum in the world. As for me... well, I am 32, so I guess I'll have to cope on my own now!'

Bride has a child from a previous marriage

When the bride has a child by a previous relationship, most guests at the wedding will be aware of the situation, but some may not. It is as well to make a positive mention of the child in the speech made by the bride's father. This – if nothing else – prevents the raising of curious eyebrows when a small boy or girl clasps the bride and calls her 'Mummy'!

Specimen 1

'Ladies and gentlemen, there is nothing in the world that could have given more pleasure to my wife, Margaret, and to me, than seeing our youngest daughter, Belinda, looking so radiantly happy. We welcome you all here to share this special day with us.

'We know Belinda's husband, Tim, to be a kind, generous and understanding person – and not bad-looking either – so Margaret keeps telling me! As most of you know, that beautiful small girl who has been crawling around the floor, singing happily to herself for the past five minutes, is Belinda's daughter, Alison. Tim loves his new daughter very dearly. He told me, just now, that he almost wept when Alison called out, in church, "What's Mummy and Daddy doing now?" We are proud to have him as our son-in-law.

'Tim's parents, Sue and Charles, are pretty wonderful people, too. Today, they've become instant grandparents and they tell us they are really thrilled at the idea.

'It's now my pleasure to propose the toast to the bride and groom. I hope you'll all agree that I should be a little unconventional, though, and include young Alison in the toast, because she is very much a part of this marriage.

'Ladies and gentlemen, I ask you, please, to stand and raise your glasses to the long life and continued happiness of the newlyweds and their young daughter. [Pause] To Belinda and Tim – and to Alison. May God bless their lives together.'

Specimen 2

'Good evening everyone. Welcome to the wedding of Jayne and myself. Thank you all for coming and, whilst I am on the subject of thank-yous, our gratitude goes out to both sets of parents and all the staff who helped out today.

'I have to say that Jayne is the most gorgeous woman I have ever seen and I am so happy and proud that she is now my wife.

'I am going to struggle to put this next part of my speech into words. There is someone else in this room that I love as dearly as my wife... and that is Michael. Mike, Daddy is so proud of you and loves you so much. I cannot thank you enough for agreeing to be one of my two Best Men today. You have given me so much joy and happiness and I want to reassure you that both Jayne and I will be there for you whenever you need us.

'When I decided that I was going to propose, I became very scared. So scared in fact that I began shaking and went pale. Over the next few weeks I saved up and bought the ring and started to think of how to ask Jayne the most important question I would ever ask. In the end I asked you, Mike, to help me and we proposed to her together. That is very apt because it is really both of us welcoming Jayne into our lives, as a wife and a mother. It is an amazing feeling knowing how well you and Jayne get on and I know how much you both love each other. I too love *you with all my heart and both Jayne and I will try and give you the same support and guidance that we have had from our families. You are always going to be special in my eyes and that will never change.*

'And if Uncle John has given you any stories to tell about Dad, then you'd better forget them quick!

'Ladies and gentlemen, please be upstanding for the two most important people in my life, Jayne and Michael!'

Illness and bereavement

It is tempting to gloss over serious or distressing subjects on what is otherwise a happy occasion. Do not do this if there is a serious illness or bereavement in either family. The facts should be acknowledged, but not dwelt upon, so that the proper respect and consideration is paid without depressing the mood.

Do not end a speech on a sad note. Try to include it somewhere in the middle so you can move back to happier themes. If you don't want to highlight who is missing then perhaps refer to it in a roundabout way by thanking the stand-in person, for example: 'Special thanks to my granddad for proudly walking me up the aisle – and keeping me at the right pace!'

Bride's father deceased

When the bride's mother is a widow, the toast to the bride and groom should be made by a relative of mature years (an uncle, for example) or an old family friend.

Specimen 1

'Ladies and gentlemen, Cheryl's mother, Sheila, has done me the great honour of asking me to propose a toast to the bride and groom.

'When I asked why I was chosen, Sheila said, "Well, you have known Cheryl since she was in Babygros!" Which, I suppose, is as good a reason as any. I should perhaps add that David was well into flares when I first met him!

'Both Sheila and Cheryl have asked me to mention Cheryl's father, Tom. Of course I will. Tom was a wonderful friend, husband and father. For sure, he's looking down on us today, so proud of his little girl. And also, for sure, he wouldn't want any of us to be sad on such a day. He would have told a good joke. So, here's one for him. A young maiden and a handsome farmhand were walking home along a country road one evening. The lad was carrying a chicken in one hand, a cane in the other, and leading a goat. On his back was strapped a large bucket. When they came to a dark lane, the maiden said, "I'm not going down there with you – you might try to kiss me." "How on earth could I do that?" asked the lad, "when I'm carrying all this." "Well," said the girl, "you could stick the cane in the ground, tie the goat to it, and put the chicken under the bucket!"

'Yes, you've guessed right! Both Cheryl and David are in farm management! They met at college. What David did with the chicken, I don't know, but it wasn't long before they announced their engagement. They are lovely people. They have a bright future in store. I know you will all want to join me in wishing them every happiness in their life together. So, please stand and raise your glasses to the health, happiness and prosperity of Cheryl and David. [Pause] To Cheryl and David!'

Specimen 2

'Ladies and gentleman, I should like to propose a toast to the happy couple. As Katie's uncle, I am so proud of what a fine young woman she has turned out to be. And I know I speak for both her mother Janice and my late brother Pete when I say how happy we are that she is marrying Karl.

'I apologise now if it gets a bit emotional. We all know that Pete would have loved to be here today but, in his absence, it's fallen to me to propose a toast for him, so, if you could all please raise your glasses, and join me in drinking to Pete. Cheers!'

Tribute to a deceased relative

When the father of the bride is very recently deceased, the bride's mother may decide that there should be a short tribute to him before the main speeches. Such a tribute would be appropriate should any close relative die just prior to the wedding. It is best made by a friend of the family.

Specimen 1

'Ladies and gentlemen, Jack's family have asked me to say a few words at this point, and I'm glad to do so. Everyone knows that Jack was so looking forward to this day. Sadly, this was not to be. Perhaps we can remember him in two ways. First by a quiet moment and then by going ahead with the reception, just as he would have wished. [Pause, head bowed, for about 15 seconds]

'This world is a better place for Jack having been with us. Our lives are richer for knowing him. [Pause] And now, ladies and gentlemen, let us go ahead with Sally and Mark's big day.'

Alternatively, the relative or friend proposing the toast to the bride and groom may be asked to pay tribute to the bride's late father in his speech.

Specimen 1

'Ladies and gentlemen, It is an honour and a great pleasure to be here to help Virginia – or Gina, as most of us know her – and Tony to celebrate their marriage.

'As many of you know, Gina's late father, Carl, was my kid brother. Many was the happy hour we spent, kicking a football around, or sparring at the gym, when we were younger. I remember I was with Carl when Gina brought Tony home to meet the family. We all got on so well. I know Carl was so looking forward to the wedding.

'Today, we are fulfilling his wishes for Gina and Tony. He is with us in our hearts and in our memories.

'Tony has been a marvellous friend to the family, always ready to help and give his advice. I know how highly Gina's mother, Marie, thinks of him. And so do we all.

'As for Gina, well, how very beautiful she looks! The family is proud of her. We all believe that she and her husband have a wonderful life ahead of them. Do remember though, Gina, the words of A. P. Herbert: "The critical period in matrimony is breakfast time!" Over the years, I have spent several breakfast times with Gina. Let's be generous and say that she is one of those people who takes a while to wake up properly in the mornings!

'Virginia – Gina – and Tony, all of us here want to wish you a long, happy, healthy and prosperous future together.

'So, ladies and gentlemen, will you please stand and join me in this toast. [Pause] To Gina and Tony!'

> ## Tip
> Remember to wait for silence before starting the toast, as you don't want to be drowned out by scraping chairs.

Bride and bridegroom living together

Nowadays, many couples live together before getting married. The groom may want to acknowledge this (specimen 1) or the bride's father may well wish to face the facts and show his complete acceptance of them, by the way his speech is worded (specimen 2).

Specimen 1

'Welcome everyone to our wedding, we are so glad you can be here to share it with us. Patsy and I have been together for about 14 years (as has been mentioned a number of times tonight) and during that time we've been through a lot. We have also had many, many good times and tradition dictates that I now tell you an amusing story or two about Patsy... fortunately she dictates that I do no such thing. But I will say, that we've been living together now for nearly eight years, and in that time I've learned a very valuable lesson: Whenever I'm wrong – admit it! Whenever I'm right – keep quiet! That's good advice for most men actually!

'Someone once told me that a successful marriage requires falling in love many times, always with the same person. I think this is true, certainly of being in a relationship at any rate and I have already fallen in love with Patsy a million times over. I look forward to falling in love with her... as my wife.'

Specimen 2

'Ladies and gentlemen, today is Karen and Philip's big day. The world belongs to them and we are here to join in the celebrations.

'As most of you will know well, Karen and Philip are very independent young people. They even insisted on making all the wedding arrangements themselves, and, what's more, on footing the bill! Wasn't that marvellous of them?

'When, two years ago, the pair of them decided they would become life partners, we of the older generation – Patricia and I, and Philip's parents, Sylvia and Jim – were just a bit concerned. Would it last, we wondered. But our fears were unfounded. I certainly don't know of a happier couple.

'Since then, their careers have gone from strength to strength and every spare moment has gone into making their new flat a real home. Obviously, they're good for each other.

'A few months ago, Philip called in one evening. He said he'd left Karen fixing up shelves because he had something important to ask me. It turned out that he'd come round to formally ask for Karen's hand in marriage. Nothing could have pleased me more. When I told Patricia – and when she had stopped weeping with joy – she said, "Do you know, they're already the most married couple I've ever seen."

'Today, knowing each other's strengths and weaknesses well, they signed the marriage contract. My job as father of the bride is to propose a toast to them. This I do with great pride. Ladies and gentlemen, will you please raise your glasses to Karen and Philip to join me in wishing them long life and good health, success in all they do, and may the happiness they have shared be continued for ever after. [Pause] To Karen and Philip.'

Bride's mother or a female friend makes the toast

There is no reason, except tradition, why the person proposing the toast to the bride and bridegroom has to be male. There are situations where the bride's mother is the obvious choice as speechmaker. Perhaps the bride's parents are divorced and her father – for whatever reason – is not at the wedding. The bride's mother could have recently remarried and, by making the speech herself, she could avoid the father or stepfather problem. Or, the bride and groom could simply request that she makes the speech, rather than a male relative.

Again, in this modern age, the bride may ask a close friend – perhaps her chief bridesmaid – to make the toast. Provided that all involved are happy with this and don't feel neglected or rejected, a close female friend makes a good choice as proposer of the toast.

Specimen 1

'Ladies and gentlemen, dear friends, welcome to all of you. How pleased we are to see you all here, joining us in celebrating the marriage of Melissa and Duncan.

'As most of you will know, Melissa is my dear daughter, and because we have always been so close, she and Duncan begged me to make the opening speech. I was, and am, absolutely thrilled at the idea.

'Melissa and I have been on our own since she was a very small girl. I am sure she will agree, we have had a good life together, not only as mother and daughter, but also as best chums. I even knew that Duncan was the right man for her before she knew it herself, and I really am happy to find that, today, I not only have a super daughter, but I've also got a super son-in-law too.

'And, I've acquired a whole new family! Duncan's parents, Maria and Bill, have adopted me into their lives; I have much to thank them for – not least for all their willing help in making this day such a success. Thank you both!

'Now, I'm supposed to offer the bride and groom advice and words of wisdom. I had looked out a suitable quotation, but as we left the Registrar's this afternoon, the sun suddenly broke through and lit up the happy faces of my daughter and her husband. And, the thought that came to my mind at that moment has replaced the quotation as my wish for them both.

'Dear Melissa, dear Duncan, whether the clouds threaten or the sun shines, hold on to your love and be as happy, always, as you are today.

'Ladies and gentlemen, please rise and join me in the toast to the bride and groom. [Pause] To Melissa and Duncan.'

Specimen 2

'Friends, it will probably seem strange to you that a chief bridesmaid is making the speech proposing the toast to the bride and groom. Jacqui particularly wanted me to do this, because of all her friends, I've known her the longest and best, and because, as she is always reminding me, I never stop talking, so I might as well use this to good effect!

'Jacqui and I met in our prams about 24 years ago. We played together as toddlers and were always in the same class at school. She was always a beautiful girl, kind, friendly and rarely flustered. I was a tomboy and usually rushing around in one panic situation or another. Yet we were inseparable.

'That is, until Will came on the scene. Then it became, Will this, and Will that, and Will's going to become this, that, and the other. I was quite sure it wouldn't last – especially when this handsome young man went off to college – and I stood by, in true pal's fashion, to pick up the inevitable pieces when the romance came to a halt.

'But, as you all know, it didn't halt at all. Jacqui and I went to work for the "Listening Bank"; Will finished college and went stockbroking in the city; and all was letters, whispered phone calls and rushing up to town for concerts, film and cuddles in the park.

'But that was my life! What Jacqui and Will got up to, I've never found out, but just a year ago they announced their engagement. Most of us here today went to their celebration party, and it was there – so I've been told – that I promised to be chief bridesmaid and to make this speech. It must have been quite a party!

'As usual, I've been chatting on and on, but I do want to be absolutely serious for a moment. In all sincerity, Jacqui and Will, I wish you all the good luck and happiness in the world. And I'm sure that, you, their friends, will echo that wish by joining me in the toast to the newlyweds.

'Will you all please stand and raise your glasses. [Pause] To Jacqui and Will – good luck and happiness, always.'

Stand-in speaker

Alternatively, someone else may want to make a speech, such as godparents, step-parents, brother or sister, a family friend or a special guest.

Specimen 1

'I am delighted to be here and feel very privileged to have been Cora's stepfather for the last 15 years. Ladies and gentlemen, I'd like to thank you all for being here today to witness the marriage of Cora and Paul. Today would not have been possible without the generous help of both sets of parents, Ken and Angela, and Fred and Jane. I know that the couple are very grateful to them.

'I know that Ken and Angela are very proud of their daughter Cora. She has worked extremely hard to get to where she is today as a qualified nurse and she is a beautiful bride. However, I will always remember her as a mischievous adolescent. She stands before us today though, as radiant on the inside as she is on the outside, a generous, warm-hearted and loving woman.

'I am not only delighted for Cora on her wedding day, but also for Paul. He is a good man and I know that Ken and Angela are delighted to welcome him into their family. Cora and Paul make a beautiful couple and they have a lot in common.

'I wish you all the happiness in the world, from the whole family. Ladies and gentlemen, please raise your glasses to Cora and Paul!'

Specimen 2

'*I feel very honoured to stand here and speak on behalf of my father, who would have loved to see my sister, Nicola, marry John. I know how delighted Nicola and John are to see so many of their friends and relatives on their special day.*

'*John, you are the perfect man for Nicola. You are kind, warm-hearted and generous, and she deserves nothing less. On behalf of my mother Irene and my father Fred, I am delighted to welcome you into the family. You have made us all proud.*

'*I would like to raise a toast to Mr and Mrs Goodman.*'

Distinguished guest

At some larger weddings, a distinguished guest who knows the bride and/or the bridegroom well, may be invited to speak at some length. He or she might be someone respected in, say, the business or academic world, or perhaps a member of the clergy, or a sports or entertainment personality. In such cases, the distinguished guest's speech is normally the only speech as such that is made. With the conventional three or four speeches, followed by a long speech, the reception would be more like a seminar! Instead, the conventional speeches are replaced by just a few words and the appropriate toast or reply. At the end of the best man's brief reply for the bridesmaids, he should introduce the distinguished guest. He or the bridegroom should say a few words of thanks at the end of the speech.

Not all people who might be regarded as distinguished guests are experienced in public speaking. Those who are, may well have never been asked to make a wedding speech before. The following specimen speech is for them, and may also provide ideas for others, preparing their own, shorter speeches.

Specimen 1

'Ladies and gentlemen, it is always a pleasure for me to attend a wedding, especially when I know the bride and groom so well. Today, I feel particularly honoured, since I have been asked to speak as a distinguished guest.

'Somewhere in this speech I'm supposed to say words of wisdom to the happy couple. It did occur to me that, like most people who fill in forms or sign contracts, Michael and Andrea may not have read the small print of the marriage contract. I see some heads nodding in agreement.

'Of course, the problem is that there's so little written at all, let alone in small print. There's no party of the first part, as in the famous Marx Brothers' sketch, and certainly no sanity clause, as when Chico says "You gotta be kidding, boss. There ain't no Sanity Clause!"

'Some people would say there ought to be a sanity clause in the marriage contract! Or at least a Government health warning! Maybe a FIMBRA-type notice saying shares can go down as well as up!

'With that in mind, I set out to survey the words of the wedding service to see just what people let themselves in for. I'm using the 1662 version of Cranmer's Prayer Book, for those who still care about such things, rather than the more recent computerised version, known as Series 3.

'For example, the Banns. These were designed, originally, to deter dowry hunters, carpetbaggers and small-time Jack the lads. They told 17th-century swingers that you don't have to put a rope round your neck in order to ring the bell a few times!

'Marriage is not to be taken lightly or wantonly. Lovely old word, "wantonly". Reminds me of the schoolboys asking a spinster schoolteacher, "Please Miss, what's a harlot?" "A harlot is, er, er, a wanton woman." "Right Miss! We all know what she's wanton!"

'We're told that marriage is ordained for procreation, but to prevent fornication! A subtle difference. Followed by words about those not having the gift of continency getting married. Strange doctrine! Sounds like: don't get married unless you have to.

'Wilt thou have this woman...? "Wilt" is what some blokes do! Or, as at the proverbial Murphy's wedding, when the priest says, "Wilt thou have this woman?" and Murphy says, "I will if nobody else will!"

'If ever there was an urgent need under the Trades Description Act, at least for a Government health warning, the marriage vows should be the prime candidate. I imagine today's happy couple didn't read the small print when they signed the register. No doubt they were so over the moon that they didn't read between the lines. I know none of us has, but that's no excuse! So following the old adage that the grass is always greener on the other side of the fence because that's where you've just come from, let's have a rather light-hearted look at what we let ourselves in for when we jumped over that moon and into the unknown.

'To start with, the vows are first spoken by the poor chap himself, the groom. Is his mind clearly on the job, as you might say, when he says: "I (and says his name) take thee, (and says the bride's name) for my wedded wife."? How on earth does he know what it means to have a wife? Perhaps all bridegrooms should read Francis Bacon. He said, amongst numerous other things: "Wives are young men's mistresses; companions for middle age; and old men's nurses."

'For better for worse, for richer for poorer. This sounds heroic. It has also been misheard as an invitation to polygamy, allowing either spouse up to 16 partners, as in four better, four worse!

'In sickness and in health. Well, it's a good idea to make sure you've both got a BUPA card!

'To love and to cherish, 'til death us do part, according to God's holy ordinance. That's fine if it just refers to the pair of us. But do I have to take on board your ravenous family and their dreadful feuds?

'Obedience is rarely mentioned these days. No wonder – the woman used to promise to obey, but didn't. The man didn't but did!

'And thereto I plight thee my troth. By the time you reach these words or their modern equivalent, it's too late. By my troth, what a plight thou art in now!

'Of course, the real crunch comes with the final pledge made by the groom alone. With this Ring, I thee wed. That's all right I suppose, except that the word ring has a capital R, which really means with all my capital, real, borrowed or mortgaged, I thee wed!

'With my body I thee worship. This isn't as obvious as the adolescent humorists think. It means, to get married, a man's body needs a thick skin, a broad back and a malleable posterior!

'And finally, With all my worldly goods I thee endow. These medieval words need updating, but surprise, surprise, they haven't been updated. That's because they appear to mean

"What's mine is yours"! And here, as so often, there's a hidden meaning. The hidden meaning is that what's mine is yours, but just you try getting your hands on it! More to the point, only the groom spoke these words! That's because the law of the land at that time, 1662, assumed that the woman not only had no property, but she was property. Which of course is why the bride's father "gives her away" to the groom.

'Seriously though, I'm sure we are all agreed that Andrea and Michael have made the right choice in choosing each other.

'So, here's to Andrea and Michael.

'Long may they keep open house to three of the best friends they'll ever have: Love, Life and Laughter!

'Ladies and gentlemen, please be upstanding and join me in a toast to [pause] the bride and groom.'

Second marriages

When the bride, or groom, or both, are marrying for the second time, being widowed or divorced, the toast to the couple is normally made by a male friend, ideally the best man, if there is one (see page 34). It is not good form to refer to earlier marriages in detail. The speech is usually quite short.

The reply by the bridegroom is traditionally the only other speech made at a second wedding and, again, may be quite short, although this is another changing convention.

Specimen 1

'Ladies and gentlemen, it is a great pleasure for me to propose the health of Sandra and Ray. All marriages are special. *Second marriages are doubly so. They are a time for renewed hope.*

'I think all of us here today were really delighted when Sandra and Ray named the day. We'd all realised a long time ago that they were so well suited. We began to think that they'd never realise it themselves.

'Ray, you said to me earlier today that you both knew how fortunate you are to have found another chance of happiness. We believe you will find that happiness. We wish you all that life can offer and hope that "the best is yet to come".

'Let us raise our glasses, then, to the bride and groom and to their happy future together. Ladies and gentlemen, [Pause] *to Sandra and Ray.'*

Specimen 2

'Ladies and gentlemen, friends, my wife and I are so pleased to see you all here, sharing our day with us. We thank you for your good wishes and for your understanding. And we are very grateful for your kind and generous gifts.

'Sandra and I were a bit overcome when my dear daughter and son-in-law, Elizabeth and Alistair, insisted that we hold our wedding reception in their lovely home. We thank you both for the loving thought. And Sandra insists that I thank you both, publicly, for taking her young daughter, Karen, to your hearts. It is wonderful that we are, already, such a close and happy family.

'Long may we continue so. And may all of you here today, meet with us on many future happy occasions. Thank you!'

Toasts at a very small, informal reception

When there is only a handful of guests at an informal reception – perhaps in a small restaurant or a pub – a very brief toast may be considered more appropriate. This can be made by the bride's father, the best man or anyone who knows the couple well. The bridegroom's reply may be just a few words of thanks.

Specimen 1

'I would like to propose a toast to Julie and Nigel, to wish them every happiness in their life together. May all your troubles be little ones! [Pause] To Julie and Nigel.'

Specimen 2

'Here's to the prettiest, here's to the wittiest,
Here's to the truest of all who are true,
Here's to the neatest one, here's to the sweetest one,
Here's to them, all in one – here's to you both.'

Specimen 3

'May you share everything, including the housework.'

Specimen 4

'It is written: when children find true love, parents find true joy. Here's to your joy and ours, from this day forward.'

Specimen 5

'Let us toast the health of the bride
Let us toast the health of the groom
Let us toast the person that tied
Let us toast every guest in the room.'

Specimen 6

'My greatest wish for the two of you is that through the years your love for each other will so deepen and grow, that years from now you will look back on this day, your wedding day, as the day you loved each other the least.'

Index